A YEAR LIKE NO OTHER

A YEAR LIKE NO OTHER

Life on a Low Income during COVID-19

Ruth Patrick, Maddy Power, Kayleigh Garthwaite,
Jim Kaufman, Geoff Page, Katie Pybus

In partnership with Covid Realities participants

First published in Great Britain in 2022 by

Policy Press, an imprint of
Bristol University Press
University of Bristol
1-9 Old Park Hill
Bristol
BS2 8BB
UK
t: +44 (0)117 374 6645
e: bup-info@bristol.ac.uk

Details of international sales and distribution partners are available at
policy.bristoluniversitypress.co.uk

British Library Cataloguing in Publication Data
A catalogue record for this book is available from the British Library

ISBN 978-1-4473-6469-6 paperback
ISBN 978-1-4473-6470-2 ePub
ISBN 978-1-4473-6471-9 ePdf

The right of Ruth Patrick, Maddy Power, Kayleigh Garthwaite, Jim Kaufman,
Geoff Page and Katie Pybus to be identified as authors of this work has been asserted
by them in accordance with the Copyright, Designs and Patents Act 1988.

Cover design: Tom Flannery
Front cover image: Emma French

Bristol University Press and Policy Press use environmentally
responsible print partners.

Printed and bound in Great Britain by CMP, Poole

This book is dedicated to every child currently experiencing poverty, and to their parents and carers struggling to get by.

Contents

List of figures and artwork credits

Figures

Artwork credits

Covid Realities participants have kindly agreed for their zine illustrations to be featured as follows:

Chapter opening illustrations created for the book by Tom Flannery.

Charting a year in a pandemic

2020

4 March ✳ The first person dies of COVID-19 in the UK.

11 March ● The World Health Organization names COVID-19 a pandemic.

20 March ● All schools across the UK are closed to all but the children of key workers and children classed as vulnerable.

Chancellor Rishi Sunak announces the furlough scheme and help for the self-employed.

23 March ● Prime Minister Boris Johnson announces the first English lockdown in response to COVID-19. Separate lockdowns are announced for Scotland, Wales and Northern Ireland.

7 April ● Boris Johnson is moved into intensive care after contracting COVID-19.

25 May ● Boris Johnson's Chief Adviser Dominic Cummings gives a statement to the press in the rose garden of Downing Street seeking to explain why his travel from London to the North East at height of lockdown was justified.

23 June	Boris Johnson says that the UK's "national hibernation" is ending and announces the relaxing of restrictions and the 2m social distancing rule.
4 July	The UK's first local lockdown comes into force in Leicester and parts of Leicestershire.
3 August	The Eat Out to Help Out scheme is launched.
11 August	Scottish schools start to reopen. Welsh, Northern Ireland and English schools follow.
14 September	The Rule of Six comes into force in England; similar restrictions are in place across the UK.
5 November	The second national lockdown comes into force in England.
23 November	AstraZeneca and Oxford University report their vaccine provides good levels of protection.
2 December	The second national lockdown ends in England and is replaced by three-tier system.
19 December	Boris Johnson tightens the rules for Christmas celebrations; parts of London and the South East have a strict 'stay at home' message.

2021

4 January — Boris Johnson says children should return to school. They return for just one day.

6 January — The third national lockdown begins in England.

22 February — Boris Johnson announces a four-stage roadmap for lifting lockdown in England.

23 February — Scottish First Minister Nicola Sturgeon announces the planned route out of lockdown.

3 March — Rishi Sunak announces a six-month extension of the £20 uplift to Universal Credit.

25 March — Welsh First Minister Mark Drakeford announces that the 'stay local' restrictions will be lifted.

29 March — The 'stay at home' message ends in England but people are encouraged to stay local.

2022

Over 10.7 million cases of COVID-19 to date and more than 146,000 deaths.

... a study like this will be part of history. It will be part of university papers and archives. Students will read our experiences as I once read and studied about the history of the welfare state, how the government failed its people ... People like to look back on history and read the diaries of real people, telling their real stories and experiences of the troubles that history books mark by dates and policies. To the future people who read this study, who read about the plights of us low-income families, know that I thank you for taking time to look back on our nation's past. And heed this: learn from our mistakes. Value your undervalued ... Maybe one day my children or grandchildren might read this study, might see these articles. Maybe someone will read about the woman who cries over bread ... Perhaps people can learn from our voices ... I'd be happy to be a whisper in history if in the future no one is left fearing homelessness or starvation. We have the resources. I hope the future will be more empathetic.

Victoria

Foreword
Voices for change

Covid Realities participants

Hope isn't something you feel a lot of when you're running in circles to make ends meet and jumping through the hoops of the powers that be. There isn't much time to dream of a better future, let alone actually work towards one. And a hopeless society is one that is kept too busy, too downtrodden to hope for change.

This book holds the voices, the experiences, feelings, thoughts and dreams of us – people who don't want to live a hopeless life. We are the people who came together through the Covid Realities research programme to debate and discuss and within these pages to collectively speak.

Since the start of the pandemic there has been so much uncertainty for so many households, none more so than for low-income households or those just living on the edge of the benefit system not eligible for help. Asking ourselves, day after day, how do we keep our family safe? How do we make our voices and concerns heard and taken seriously?

We have had to make impossible decisions these last 18 months, cutting back to the barest basics. Terrified about paying bills, heating our homes and about feeding our children and ourselves. Balancing where the most urgent need lies, with school uniforms to buy, technology to keep up with, no resources for activities and often limited space even for play.

Feeling ashamed to be grateful for lockdowns as birthday parties were stopped, along with the need to spend on presents we could ill afford. And, as for Christmas, how sad is it to wish your child no longer believed so you might be honest and say you cannot afford presents? All the while home schooling, protecting, some grieving, many isolated and all of us scared. Struggling to see beyond one dark moment to the next. When children are young they don't understand our situations. When they are older they should not have to.

We are exhausted. Sick of being penalised for circumstance. Every move overseen by an uncaring few. Battling judgement and expectations of gratitude for the smallest financial sticking plaster from the government, only for it to be ripped back off when deemed no longer necessary. It's never ending – the weight of trying to balance on the tightrope that low incomes and Universal Credit force so many of us to walk. Bills are ever increasing whilst household income drops like a brick. It feels like drowning. Silently asking 'can we sink any further?'

> "Not waving but drowning", why can't you see
> As SSK[1] spray paints "Tethered to Deep Poverty"?
> Same storm perhaps, but not the same boat, if you have one at all
> Help those treading water to stay safe, well & afloat.

Little changes to the system, the small asks, whilst useful, feel like a compromise, an apology for daring to speak up. Because what we really need to change is the cause, not just the symptoms. The reason things are like they are. The common thread that runs through the entire system. It feels so daunting because it is. It's a thread that once pulled would unravel so many related systems and established processes. But that doesn't mean we shouldn't pull it.

Not only do we need huge policy change, and a total shift of politics, we need people to care. We need the people who have the voice, the people who have the power, to care about the marginalised. We need them to change the narrative. A better, fairer social security system is one built on respect, dignity and equity. Decent social security needs to work with and see the humanity of those who need it. It needs to value all of us as worthy, valuable members of society.

Because perhaps the biggest, most radical, change to the social security system would be to change the way the people who need it are seen by society. If we can be seen as equals, as humans, as families just trying to make a better life for our children, if we can be seen as worthy and deserving of help and support, if we can be allowed to make mistakes and be flawed and real, then we have hope. Hope for a system that truly helps people find a way out of poverty. Hope that no child or adult goes hungry or struggles to keep a roof over their head. Hope for our children and for their children, and theirs.

The Covid Realities project has valued and listened to all of its participants. Through the programme, we have had a safe space to share our experiences, our fears, our worries. To tell our stories. Through the last 18 months our courage has been tested, pulled, tugged and twisted. Our self-worth battered and bruised. But by sticking together we are strong. Stronger. We can scream at the same time.

Over the pandemic, we have taken comfort from not being alone, inspiration from our shared resilience. This leaves us resolved that the struggles of those surviving on low incomes should not remain invisible but instead must go towards a wider awareness and change.

To this end we are proud to use our collective voice here and beyond.

We ask that you, reader, please listen and understand. And above all, join us in hoping and agitating for a better world.

Covid Realities
Words of participants curated by Laura Lindow,
December 2021

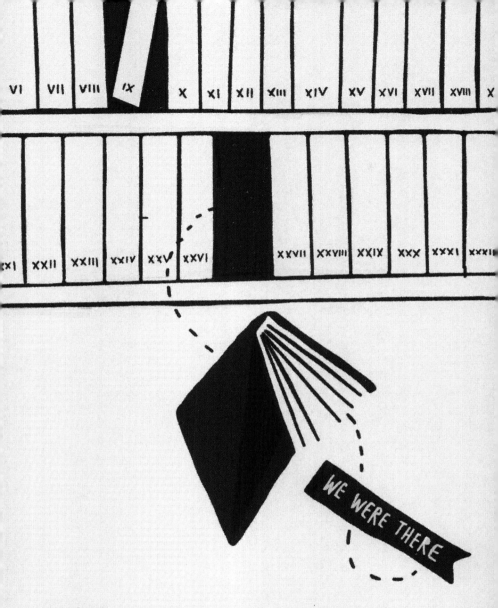

Introduction

A whisper in history:
poverty, families and the pandemic

Led by Ruth and Maddy

We made a game of walking through the leaves. We no longer had a car. His father left. But the hardship began and I was living from day to day.

I did not ever choose to be on benefits and I am always deeply offended when people say that people on benefits are living it up, we all have an easy life and luxury goods. We don't!

We walk and we budget and people buy us bags of shopping and surreptitiously put it away to save our embarrassment.

Lois

Universal Credit is the curse word at this time, how can our country say that they care when people are left struggling?

Joseph

A different take on the pandemic

In time, there will be many, many books about the COVID-19 pandemic. Some have already been written, while others are no doubt being printed as we write. In time, there will be explosive memoirs by politicians and public health officials promising a behind-the-scenes look at the biggest global crisis since the Second World War. There will be scientific analyses as well as polemics, and books that try to understand how we coped, and often didn't, with the extraordinary and sudden changes in all of our lives. This book is different. It is a book that shares voices and experiences that are too often ignored, and not just during the pandemic. These are the voices of parents and carers living in poverty and struggling, day in, day out, to get by on too little. The voices of parents and carers whose experiences of the pandemic were different because of their poverty, who faced special pressures when the fear of the virus collided with their everyday worries about trying to make ends meet. These are the voices of parents and carers who want to do the best for their children, and who have to handle the emotional and practical fallout when there's just not enough money to go around.

This book elevates these voices, sharing accounts of parents and carers, who are united both in their experiences of hardship and in their determination to make change happen. These parents and carers are the core of this book. It is their voices that matter.

All in it together? An unequal and divided nation

COVID-19 arrived in Britain following a decade of austerity, and during the chaotic drama of Brexit, the country's exit from the European Union. Caught off guard, we entered the pandemic a distracted, unequal and severely divided nation. Yet, as the virus swept across the country, when the first national lockdown was announced, and then again when the Prime Minister ended up in intensive care with COVID-19, we saw the return of an old, familiar phrase. 'COVID-19 can affect any of us', we were told. 'The virus does not discriminate. *We are all in this together.*'

While politicians tried to rally a national wartime spirit to help people through the coming months, it was clear that, although appealing, this unifying rhetoric was wide of the mark. Even at the outset of the pandemic, it was obvious that experiences of COVID-19 would be anything but equal. It was not long before evidence emerged showing a disproportionate risk of death from the virus for racially minoritised people[1] and people on the lowest incomes.

If the phrase *all in it together* seems familiar, it might have been because we remembered it from its last outing over ten years earlier. In the aftermath of another global crisis – the global financial crisis – Cameron's newly elected Conservative and Liberal Democrat coalition government announced an unprecedented and wide-reaching programme of cuts to public spending. In his victory speech on becoming Conservative Party leader, David Cameron set out his underpinning philosophy:

> 'I believe that if you trust people and give them more power and control over their lives, they become stronger, and society becomes stronger too, and I believe profoundly that we are all in this together.'

Over the next ten years, Cameron and his colleagues would return again and again to the idea of us being 'all in it together' as part of wider efforts to legitimise austerity. These cuts were necessary, it was argued, to reduce the budget deficit – the gap between government revenue and spending. In the ten years leading up to the pandemic, the budget deficit was a near-daily topic of heated political debate and discussion. Reducing the deficit was used to justify cuts to our public services, to our social security and so to the very fabric of our welfare state. This recent history is essential to understanding what happened during the pandemic, and why it happened in the way it did.

Cuts, cuts, cuts: more, more, more

During the repeated lockdowns, almost all of us watched a lot of TV. One great hit of the long lockdown months was Channel 4's *It's a Sin*, which shone a light on the HIV epidemic in the United Kingdom (UK) of the 1980s. The soundtrack was a glorious reminder of the music of that time, and I[2] often stuck the playlist on to mark the end of another week. The lyrics of 1980s band Carmel from their song 'More More More' reminded me of David Cameron and George Osborne, then Prime Minister and Chancellor of the Exchequer respectively, standing again and again at the despatch box in the House of Commons, or in large auditoriums for their annual Conservative Party conference speeches, setting out cut after cut after cut. There was the same jauntiness in their tone as in Carmel's song. In 2015, Cameron was voted back into government with his first majority government. It seemed that the British electorate's response to cuts, cuts, cuts was more, more, more. And that's exactly what we got.

The Women's Budget Group estimates that £83 billion of cuts were announced in 2010, with a further £15 billion taken from the social security budget in 2015.[3] In the decade before the pandemic, a total of 50 cuts were made to social security. These cuts came in different forms. Some removed entitlements, while others reduced levels of support.

The cuts fell unevenly, not just because the poorest households are most likely to suffer when benefit levels are cut and public service budgets reduced, but also because of political decisions about whom to protect from the worst effects of austerity. The triple lock on pensions, introduced in 2010, meant that support for pensioners would rise by whichever was the highest out of inflation, the average wage increase or 2.5%. Yet young people were frequently targeted with reductions in state support: for example, when the triple lock was introduced in 2010, the Educational Maintenance Allowance – financial support to stay in post-16 education – was scrapped.

The deficit reduction programme also fell unevenly in other ways. A balance of 85% cuts and 15% tax rises necessarily meant that those most reliant on state support felt the impact the hardest. This meant especially poor outcomes for women, racially minoritised people, disabled people and families with children. Upper middle-income households – some of those least reliant on state support and services – actually benefited from tax cuts, and saw net cash transfers from the state *to them* increase between 2010 and 2015. At the same time, the incomes of the lowest-earning households fell sharply.[4]

In stark contrast to the 'triple lock' on pensions, Alison Garnham, Chief Executive of the charity Child Poverty Action Group, warned back in 2010 that families in poverty faced a 'triple whammy' of cuts to benefits, reductions in support and advice, and disappearing public services.[5] Changes to legal aid and local authority budget cuts saw welfare rights advice services close just at a time when many needed them most. At the same time, the benefits system began to place much more emphasis on looking for work, and on monitoring and supervising people's behaviour. The expectations placed on claimants became much harsher, as did the sanctions for not meeting them. These tough new expectations and sanctions were also extended to more and more groups of claimants: to single parents with younger children; to partners in working households; and also to people in work but receiving some support through Universal Credit or the Tax Credit system.

Justifying austerity: the problem with 'welfare'

Austerity was justified by an accompanying narrative that presented it as inevitable and necessary, rather than as a political choice. The 'alchemy of austerity'[6] was to make pain and suffering appear as harsh but necessary medicine that would do its patient good. So, as social security was subjected to cut after cut, and levels of benefit support plummeted, we were told that this would correct cultures of welfare dependency and 'help' people on 'welfare' to move off benefits and into work. This story was circulated by politicians and enthusiastically amplified by the media, creating what Tracey Jensen and Imogen Tyler describe as 'anti-welfare commonsense'.[7] By 'commonsense' they mean a web of preconceptions and assumptions about the world that are taken for granted and rarely questioned. They describe a 'machine of anti-welfare commonsense' through which these assumptions are produced. The cogs in the machine are politicians, but also the media and the stories they spin. Each feeds off the other, legitimising ever more stigmatising language and distorted representations of the lives of those in receipt of social security for all or most of their income. This anti-welfare commonsense has bulldozed its way through opposition and resistance, dominating the landscape and effectively crowding out the possibility for different narratives to emerge.

We saw this in David Cameron and George Osborne's promises to fix 'broken Britain', and in their effective rebranding of social security as 'welfare'. Welfare, we were told, created dependency and problematic, intergenerational chains of worklessness. We saw it in political statements that, despite the 'all in it together' niceties, deliberately divided the population into static groups of 'hard working families' and 'welfare dependents'. Witness Cameron's first speech after becoming Prime Minister, where he set out his idea of fairness:

> 'But here is something else about fairness. Fairness isn't just about who gets help from the state. The other part of the equation is who gives that help, through their taxes. Taking more money from the man who goes out to work long hours each single day so the family next door can go on living a life on benefits without working – is that fair? No. Fairness means giving people what they deserve – and what people deserve can depend on how they behave. If you really cannot work, we will always look after you. But if you can work, and you refuse to work, we will not let you live off the hard work of others.'

The circulation of negative characterisations of benefit claimants by politicians also involved the co-opting of high-profile media cases to further stigmatise 'welfare' and the lives of those reliant on social security. We saw people convicted of child abduction and murder (Karen Matthews and Mick Philpott) held up as an exemplary illustration of the dangers of an over-generous benefits system. Politicians were happy to exploit these cases for ideological gain. David Cameron himself wrote an article in the *Daily Mail* with the headline: 'There are 5 million people on benefits in Britain: How do we stop them turning into Karen Matthews?' The provocation was clear, crude. The denigration of 'welfare' was further enabled by an explosion in programmes

described as 'Poverty Porn', shows that claim to show the realities of life on benefits, but in fact show a highly edited, partial and sensationalised depiction. There was then an endless loop of the media and politicians producing and reproducing stigmatising portrayals of welfare, and it is no coincidence that this was happening in parallel with sweeping cuts to social security support.

The austerity decade meant that Britain entered 2020 with a social security system especially ill-equipped for the challenges it was about to face.[8] Two key statistics and two broader trends are instructive here. First, at the start of the pandemic there were 4.3 million children living in poverty in the UK – one in three children. Second, Britain's largest food bank network, the Trussell Trust, handed out just shy of two million food parcels in 2019/20, 33 times more than in 2010. Likely related to these are two broader trends: infant mortality has risen over recent years, and life expectancy has stalled for the first time – something which has not occurred since 1900. In some areas, particularly in the North of England, life expectancy before the pandemic was actually falling:[9] a damning indictment on the very real human cost of the austerity years. It was against this backdrop of poverty and food bank use, of government policies that created rather than prevented destitution, that we set up the Covid Realities research project. This book is about that project, but most importantly it is about the parents and carers who took part, about their experiences and their recommendations for change. It has been written collaboratively, with each chapter pulled together by one (or in some cases two) of the researchers.

Why do we need to find out about poverty in a pandemic?

When the pandemic reached the UK in March 2020, the researchers behind this book, like everyone, experienced profound shock and uncertainty. How would the parents among us cope with school closures? And how might vulnerable family members best protect themselves from the pandemic? How could everyday life continue when nothing was the same, and all our usual activities were off limits? We all recall that time in March 2020 as one of fear, disbelief and lots and lots of questions. I recall wandering to my local corner shop in a daze, trying and failing to digest what the closure of schools meant for me, my partner and my four young children. At the shop, I looked for something to distract me from my fears. Settling on a pack of cigarettes, I hoped that an illicit smoke would help me escape (at least temporarily) from the craziness of the moment I was living through. It didn't.

But, in the midst of all the uncertainty, some things were totally clear. As researchers, we knew that families in poverty would be facing particular challenges during this time, and that these would likely only harden as the pandemic continued. We knew that families have well-developed strategies for eking out every last bit of their limited income, strategies that were suddenly made impossible because of the pandemic. We knew that the arrival of home schooling, and the expectation that people would learn 'online', would cause the biggest headaches for those with the least financial resources. People who might not have available devices or a Wi-Fi connection. We also knew there was a risk that, in the rush to respond to the pandemic, the challenges faced by families living in poverty would be neglected.

As the pandemic hit, members of the research team were variously researching the impact of recent benefit changes (Ruth), food insecurity (Kayleigh and Maddy), the fragmentation of poverty (Ruth and Kayleigh), welfare conditionality (Jim and Ruth), drug treatment services (Geoff) and the relationships between poverty and mental ill health (Katie). We wanted to continue our existing work, but also undertake new research to help document and share the experiences of families on a low income at this extraordinary and terrifying time.

Many of us had previously adopted participatory approaches to research. You will hear more about this approach as you read on, but, in short, 'participatory research' is rooted in a simple idea: research is more robust and ethical when it works *with* participants, rather than treating them as objects of scientific study. Seeing participants as potential collaborators rather than objects for investigation is essential if our research is to draw on and make use of the expertise that comes from, and ultimately can only come from, direct, personal (lived) experience. This was the impetus behind Covid Realities, a research programme that sought to do just that by working in partnership with parents and carers living on a low income across the UK during the pandemic.

What is Covid Realities?

The Covid Realities research programme began life after the Nuffield Foundation, an independent charitable trust, announced that it wanted to support research teams to rapidly respond to the pandemic. Usually, applications for research funding develop over many months, even years. In this case, the Nuffield Foundation asked researchers to pull together proposals incredibly quickly, arguing, in March 2020, that the unfolding crisis needed an immediate response. In his call for research applications, Tim Gardam,[10] the charity's Chief Executive, foresaw the likely social implications of the pandemic as it started to unfold:

> The virus may give practical expression to the rhetorical aspiration of 'solidarity' … Equally, it may just be a moment to remember. Societies are very resilient to disaster and to economic turmoil, but they are changed by them.

I recall seeing Tim's invitation pop up on my Twitter feed as I sat in my hotel room in Stockton-on-Tees, on what would be my last working night away from home for many, many months. I was in Stockton to help facilitate a workshop with Poverty2Solutions, a coalition of groups with lived experiences of poverty. At the workshop, we spoke of the constant drip-feed of news about COVID. It felt unreal and frightening. Everything about that work trip felt both routine and yet different. The hand sanitiser in the hotel lobby. The quietness on the trains. The farewells as we left the workshop, unsure when we might see each other again.

As I travelled home, I thought more about Tim's blog, and about what or how I could usefully contribute. I reached out to Alison Garnham at Child Poverty Action Group, and to

Kayleigh, who contacted Maddy to see if she would like to be involved. There was lots we felt unsure about: uncertainty a new constant in these strange times. How would the crisis unfurl, and how would our existing work have to change in response? I had collaborated with Kayleigh for a long time, while Kayleigh and Maddy were good friends through involvement in activist networks. But I had never actually met Maddy (and wouldn't do so until long into the research project). Would it be possible to establish a major research project with people who were effectively strangers? Maddy recalls going round in circles in her head over the course of a couple of hours (at this early stage we had to make decisions incredibly quickly) about whether or not she should be involved – would it be possible to balance this project with her existing work, doing justice to both?

In the end, though, all three of us felt it was essential to ensure that experiences of poverty through the pandemic were closely monitored and were part of the broader national conversation.

This meant that over an intensive few days, we (Ruth, Kayleigh and Maddy) responded to Tim's invitation. We thought about how we might best create research fit for purpose in these extraordinary times. The idea we came up with was for an online research project, working with parents and carers living on a low income to create a safe and supportive space to document experiences of the pandemic, and to develop recommendations for change. Our proposal was new and untested: pioneering, yes, but we also felt it was a little foolhardy. As we grappled with the new COVID-19 context, why were we applying to do yet more work? How would we make sure that we did not simply add more pressures to parents already struggling to get by? And how were we going to adapt our research for this new and emerging world of Zoom and working from home? When we got official notification that we'd been funded, we were both pleased that this important work could start, but also daunted. Could we deliver on what we'd proposed? And how would we ever get anything done with the children around all of the time, and amid the constant worry of the pandemic? Later on in the project we were joined by first Geoff, then Katie and Jim. What was it going to be like running a major research project together when we lived in different parts of the country, and when most of us had never even met in person?

Learning from different voices

This book, for better or worse, is a testament to our perseverance in working through these fears and challenges. But, much more importantly, it is a testament to the incredible input of the parents and carers whom we have been fortunate enough to collaborate with through Covid Realities.

Inspired by the Mass Observation Archive[11] that developed during the Second World War, we adapted its approach, making use of the different technologies now available. Over more than a year, between June 2020 and July 2021, we invited people living on a low income with children to complete online diaries and record their thoughts, feelings and everyday experiences. We didn't know how people would respond to this invitation: 'I'm far too busy', they might say, or maybe 'What's the point?' or 'Who will listen?' Many may have felt exactly that, but for more than a hundred others, their diaries became a space to share how they were feeling, and to reflect on their experiences.

Parents in Covid Realities also reacted to events in the news, and responded to weekly questions, which we called 'big questions of the week'. These were recorded on video and put directly to them by the research team, by other participants and by external guests from different organisations. We also developed monthly virtual discussion groups – what we called our 'Big Ideas' groups – where parents from all four nations of the UK could come together on Zoom to explore the problems they faced, their ideas for change and simply to share their thoughts. The 'Big Ideas' meetings were also the project's decision-making forum, the place where we agreed what to do and why. These online meetings provided parents with an unexpected, but very welcome, source of peer support that one participant, Lola, described as a "safe space to be our raw selves without putting on a front, and being around like-minded people". Many participants have spoken about how valuable this was for them, especially single parents who were locked down alone.

We mentioned earlier that, informed by our previous research, the project took a participatory approach. Taking a participatory approach (so that research is conducted with rather than on people) is especially important in the context of poverty and social security research, because people in poverty are routinely stigmatised or ignored. Although frequently spoken about, more often than not the voices of people living in poverty are not heard in popular and political debate – even on issues that directly affect them. As researchers and campaigners Nancy Fraser and Ruth Lister remind us, poverty is about social injustice. But the injustice is not just a lack of sufficient income, or the injustice of economic inequality. It is also the injustice of being routinely portrayed as somehow less than people who are not in poverty: less deserving, less productive, less effective at managing life. People in poverty routinely experience this further layer of injustice, which is often fuelled by their treatment by politicians and in the media.

At its best, participatory research with people in poverty can be a way to move towards a society that is more equal and just. It makes a space for their voices to find a way back into the conversation. Adopting participatory approaches during a pandemic has been challenging, time intensive, but also extraordinarily rewarding. We have been so fortunate to have the opportunity to collaborate with our participants, and we have sought to build from their expertise and insights at every turn.

Across the research, we have included participants in all areas of activity, involving them in key decisions and pursuing new avenues in light of their suggestions. This led directly to some arts-based activity emerging from the research, with participants coming together during three workshops with artist Jean McEwan to produce a zine (a DIY magazine) about their 'COVID realities' and hoped-for post-COVID futures. You will see images from this zine throughout the book. Participants have also been the key spokespeople for Covid Realities, taking to the airwaves to bring their experiences directly to wider public discussion about poverty and social security during the pandemic.

In the work that informed this book, we have learned from our previous participatory research (conducted face to face and in 'normal' times), adapting things for the new virtual and online world of the pandemic. We have made loads of mistakes along the way, and faced many tough choices and difficult decisions. On such occasions it has always helped to return to the ethical principles that drive us and shape our research – ideas of caring for participants and each other, of equality and mutual exchange, and of sharing. Above all, our approach can be summarised by the simple strapline: 'always sweat the small details'. We needed to spend lots of time thinking about how the spaces we created online were supportive ones, and to regularly reflect on and take time on our communications with the parents and carers we worked with.

When I run face-to-face participatory workshops, I always spend most of my time making cups of tea, checking everyone is getting their favourite type of pizza delivered (and arranging an alternative take-out for those few people who don't like pizzas). This is partly about ensuring that people are well looked after during the workshop, but it is also about changing the power dynamics, placing myself in the role of supporting the participants' work. Shifting online, we sought to keep this approach, adapting it for the new context. We sent out what became known as 'snack packs' before each of our 'Big Ideas' groups. These packs, kindly made up by Teresa Frank, our brilliant project support worker at the University of York, included snacks to keep children occupied, hot chocolate sachets and biscuits. The act of pulling together and sending these snack packs was a simple, everyday expression of our ethics of care, and demonstrated the importance we placed on participants and their involvement in Covid Realities.

Alongside care, we also tried to put ideas of equality and mutual exchange into practice. This approach informed the way we conducted the 'Big Ideas' groups, and how we asked the 'big questions of the week' that we sent out to participants by email. In the group, and when asking questions of participants, the research team openly shared their own experiences of the COVID-19 pandemic too.

A bit about the book

Across this book, you'll hear directly from Covid Realities parents and carers who will share their experiences with you, and will tell you about their everyday life during an extraordinary year.[12] This book contains extracts both from individual diary accounts and also from answers to 'big questions of the week'. These entries have all been anonymised, with participants choosing their own alias. Each chapter opens with narratives written by participants specifically for inclusion in this book. Some of these include participants' real first names, but some people preferred to use their alias for these, too. This may sound needlessly complicated but it has been about giving participants choice and control over their anonymity, and recognising that people often feel differently in different contexts and that it is our job as researchers to realise and respect these preferences.

We have worked directly with participants to develop and write this book, and they have driven key decisions, specifically, for example, the chronological structure that takes you through a year in a pandemic from March 2020 – a year none of us ever expected, or wanted, to see. We take readers back to the early days of the first lockdown, when the sun constantly shone over our new dystopian world: a world of being allowed out of the house only once a day; of long hours trying to find an online shopping spot; and of struggling to get to grips with home schooling. We take readers through the pandemic Christmas, the temporary lifting of restrictions and the rush to see families and friends, to have a special (or even an ordinary) Christmas at a time when life was anything but ordinary. Then we move on to what was for so many an especially bleak time – to the third lockdown, and to a seemingly endless and relentless winter.

Our chronological structure allows us to explore how key moments in the pandemic were experienced by families on a low income over the course of the year. However, we have also used each chapter to pull out key themes from across the 12 months – for example, the increased strain around getting by on benefits; the relationship between financial strain and mental ill health; or the inequalities that shaped people's experience of the pandemic. This approach, both chronological and highlighting key issues and experiences for families on a low income, allows us to build a rich, detailed picture of lives lived across the pandemic. Focusing on the first year of the pandemic alone allows us to provide this level of detail. It also means that we can make sure that what we have found is shared – as quickly as possible – to contribute to conversations for change. We know that the pandemic wasn't yet over by the end of the 12 months documented here. In fact, it wasn't even over at the time of writing, and from today's vantage point it's hard to say what 'over' would actually mean. But those first 12 months were an extraordinary time for many people, and we feel it is vital to share just how hard life has been for families on a low income, in the hope that we can all use this knowledge to make sure that future years are better. We hope that lessons can be learned from the first year of the pandemic in the UK.

In writing and then editing this book, we have been reminded of the extraordinary times we have all lived through (and are still living through), and the historically significant changes we have seen both to everyday lives and also in the scale and nature of government intervention. At times, we have found writing this book to be distressing, having to take ourselves back to periods of time that were difficult personally, and that hold upsetting memories that in many ways we would rather forget. But we have also been energised by our memories of our work with the Covid Realities participants, of 'Big Ideas' groups, where participants shared encounters and laughs, a bleak, dark humour often running through their accounts of getting by without very much, and of feeling adrift from the mainstream narratives about the pandemic.

The people behind Covid Realities

This book has been written collaboratively and draws extensively on participants' own accounts as recorded in diary entries and other research activities. It also includes some reflections from the research team about their own experiences.

As a team of authors we have faced various (and different) challenges during the pandemic, and have talked about some of these across the book. You will hear our different voices coming through in the chapters, with different authors leading the writing of each. More importantly, however, you will hear the voices of Covid Realities participants. There is a bit of a tension in this book around us wanting both to focus very squarely on the accounts of people in poverty during the pandemic – what really matters – and also to share some personal reflections from our own lives. Our main aim is to share what life was like on a low income for families in the pandemic. Nonetheless, we blend in our own personal reflections in the hope that they help capture both the process of working on Covid Realities and also the extraordinary realities we have all lived through during this pandemic. Sharing some of our own experiences also links to the ethics of reciprocity – of sharing and mutuality, discussed previously – that underpins our approach across the project. Just as the participants are sharing their accounts and everyday realities, so we are sharing some of ours; just as they are giving a bit of themselves, we are giving a bit of ourselves. This also mirrors what we did together in the 'Big Ideas' groups, where all of us – participants and researchers alike – shared our own COVID realities for the day at the start of each online meeting.

What all this means is that, reading this book, you will encounter lots of different people, and lots of different voices. To help you keep track of these, here you will find brief pen portraits of some of the participants who feature most frequently throughout the book. These pen portraits are written by the participants themselves, and there are also pen portraits of each of the authors.

> AURORA: Desperately hoping for change. Struggling, solo parent of two children.
>
> BRIAN: I am a single-parent father living on a low income with my daughter of school age. I am not asking for change solely for my own benefit. I ask for change, as many people do, so our children can grow up in a caring and equal society so they have the best possible chance to make the best of their future lives and reach their full potential without feeling disadvantaged and not as appreciated as others in better financial and stable positions.

CAROLINE: I am a mum first, that is my most important job in life, and a childcare provider. I am a fighter and a strong believer in a society that values and respects everyone. I am a strong advocate for speaking up and teaching our young children how to question things and to look at the world with empathy and consideration. We never know what is going on in anyone else's life and mind.

DEIRDRE: I am a single mother of two children, a boy age 8 and a girl age 12. I am a qualified teacher but due to domestic violence and looking after my mental health I am now on Universal Credit trying to get well enough to apply for work again.

ELLA: Media Spokesperson and Ambassador, gentle mother to twin daughters Bella and Ruby, age 3. Love travelling, boxing and football.

EMDAD: I am a dad of 3 children who enjoys spending time with them, visiting local attractions and helping them with their homework, as well as teaching them the etiquette and manners to live in a diverse community. I believe that this life is short and whatever you get in your life, try to stay happy and help others who need it. This is the way we can give something back to our communities where we were raised and grown up.

EMMA: I am 28 years old, happily married with three children, I have always worked up until some unfortunate events landed me on benefits.

FAITH: Divorced, loved daughter and Mum of two. Never look back, your future is waiting for you!!

GEOFF: As I grow older, I have become increasingly semi-social. Because of this, lockdown provided some real peace for me, my (single parented) 7-year-old, and two Labradors. Home schooling PLUS full-time work has often been brutal; but there have been moments of quietness and benefits, too.

JIM: I live in Sheffield with my wife, Kat, and our
two young children. When all this started we
were living in Glasgow. COVID turned our lives
upside down!

JO: Mum to a beautiful boy with SEN [special
educational needs]. I'd love a workplace and a
society that supported him and my care of him,
proudly. Found myself on benefits after a successful
career and travelling the world. Let me tell you,
it's harsh.

JOSEPH: I am 46, disabled with a wife and 3 children,
my eldest who is Autistic. I am on legacy benefits.
I am working part time with my housing provider
and volunteer nationally and locally with regard
to housing rights and what we want to see from
the government. I feel passionate about change
for the better.

KATIE: I live in York with my husband, John, a pub
landlord. Like many in the hospitality sector, the
pandemic brought lots of uncertainty for us and
we missed family, friends and the pub community.
We did end up with a lovely dog called Frank,
though, which was one positive.

KAYLEIGH: I live in County Durham with my husband,
Craig. I really missed my 95-year-old Gran during
lockdown, but living next door to my Mam meant
(socially distanced) backyard coffees, which helped
get me through the repeated lockdowns!

KIM: I'm a mother to 4 sons and married. Life
was settled until COVID stole my husband's
job. I hope that reading our stories helps you to
understand our plight and encourages you to do
your own research.

MADDY: I live in York with my partner, Sky, and our
seven-week-old baby. Lockdown meant furlough
for Sky, who works in a bookshop. But he was
soon busy, painting our house from top to bottom.
And then repainting it when we decided a bright
red kitchen was a bit much!

Rosie: A mum of 3. Passionate about social justice and mental health awareness.

Ruth: I live in Bradford with four young children and my partner, Martin. The pandemic meant interruptions to Martin's work (he's an electrician) and endless, endless lockdowns and bubbles bursting, given high rates and extra local restrictions in Bradford.

Shirley: Disabled Lone Parent, Carer, Activist, Expert by Experience & Covid Realities Participant.

Victoria: I'm a single parent, domestic violence and childhood abuse survivor. I was raised under the poverty line, by a single mum who took her anger at the world out on me. What do I want you to know about me? I won't let my children grow up as scared and hungry as I was. The cycle needs to end, not just for my children but for all our children.

Together, we have created this book. It is these voices that you will hear as we go back to the beginning of the pandemic, and to what was a year like no other. We hope that this book gives you a window into these individual lives: lives that are so far removed from the simplified cardboard cut-out representations of benefit claimants that still feature regularly in media accounts, and which sometimes seem to play a role in informing government policy. We also hope that the future will be a better one, for all of us, and that there will be public will to build a social security system capable of helping people in moments of need. In times like the pandemic, but also in more ordinary times: when children are born, when work dries up, when ill health falls. The social security system should be there for everyone. Its failure to be there in any adequate way both before and during the pandemic is a failure that positively screams out from this book. We hope you hear the scream; and pass the scream (or even better this book) on to others. Together, perhaps we can create enough noise to make real change possible.

Chapter one
Britain enters lockdown

Led by Kayleigh

There was nothing that could have prepared us for lockdown. It felt like eternity. Lucky were those who had Wi-Fi. But stuck in a [women's] refuge where Wi-Fi was hard to come by, let alone visitors, our mental health was really getting the best of us. You look out the window and just think, 'You lucky dog owners, you can just walk out the house, not looking who's behind you, or take your child for a bike ride.' Freedom looks very different when you are inside a refuge. Some might call it minimised living. Others, like my grateful self, would declare the refuge an escape to freedom.

Angie

They announced the pandemic on the news. They said we had to lock down but there was no DIRECTION! No sense. The news was so loud. I fell down slowly.

Lois

Introduction

Across 2020 and well into 2021, repeated lockdowns meant we saw much less of the people that matter most to us. Social contact with parents, grandparents, friends, work colleagues – even small talk with people at a bus stop, or at the next table in a cafe – was suddenly and drastically restricted. But as our social worlds narrowed (and often darkened), many of us received more communications from politicians than we'd ever known. The need to inform the nation about the steps we were being asked to take to 'stay safe, protect the NHS, save lives' led to daily briefings and televised set pieces by an awkwardly sombre Boris Johnson, searching for Churchillian stature and unifying rhetoric.

It was Boris Johnson who repeatedly appeared on television in our living rooms in March 2020 as all of our lives changed suddenly, and beyond recognition. 'Social distancing.' 'Quarantine.' 'Furlough.' 'Lockdown.' 'Self-isolation.' 'Herd immunity.' 'Bubbles.' These words and phrases rapidly became part of our everyday life, taking on new and often frightening meanings. Empty shelves in the supermarket reflected the fear, uncertainty and panic that COVID-19 had created. People sold hand sanitiser on eBay for 50 times more than its original price as everyone frantically tried to protect themselves. Essential household shopping items such as baked beans, rice and toilet rolls rose in price by 4.4% in April 2020 alone.[1]

Connie, a Covid Realities participant, wrote in her diary that life changed from '0 to 100', as the government shut down businesses and schools, and restricted people from leaving their homes. For those that could, home working meant setting up laptops on kitchen tables and in bedrooms. Others had to enter the workplace with the worry of possibly contracting the virus and bringing it home to their families. People in precarious, low-paid, manual jobs in the caring, retail and service sectors were more exposed to COVID-19 as their face-to-face jobs had to continue.[2] Often, people in these jobs were classed as key workers, on the front line in the fight against coronavirus.

It's pretty traumatic thinking back to March 2020, when I[3] was so terrified of coronavirus that I spent £20 on some disinfecting wipes on eBay as the shops were all sold out. This sort of inflated pricing meant many families couldn't afford to access the essentials they needed to live on. In those early days of the pandemic, none of us knew just how much coronavirus would impact on the world, or on our day-to-day lives. At the beginning, Boris Johnson assured us it would all be over within 12 weeks. This offered (false) hope, which created yet more fear and uncertainty when it went unfulfilled. Would coronavirus be with us for months, years, forever? At the beginning, there were lots of questions, but no answers. But something that did become clear very quickly was that it wasn't going to affect everyone equally. And families living on low incomes faced particular challenges from the very beginning of the pandemic.

Lockdown and the everyday challenges of getting by

On the evening of Monday, 23 March 2020, Prime Minister Boris Johnson announced what was to become known as the first 'lockdown', featuring some of the strictest restrictions on freedom the UK had ever seen. Exercise was allowed for only one hour a day. We had to stand two metres apart from people we didn't live with. Shopping was for essential items only. The lockdown was supposed to last for three weeks. But what actually happened was a seemingly never-ending series of lockdowns, either national or local, that continued to affect the UK well into 2021, causing upheaval, uncertainty and unpredictability. Tiered systems of restrictions across not only the devolved nations but also regionally shone a light on place-based inequalities in Britain, a country more geographically unequal than any other rich nation.[4]

On the next page is an extract from Johnson's speech with what he termed 'very simple instruction(s)'. For families on a low income, these restrictions challenged not only their freedoms but also their strategies for getting by.

From this evening I must give the British people a very simple instruction – **you must stay at home.**

Because the critical thing we must do is stop the disease spreading between households.

That is why people will only be allowed to leave their home for the following very limited purposes:

- shopping for basic necessities, as infrequently as possible;
- one form of exercise a day – for example a run, walk, or cycle – alone or with members of your household;
- any medical need, to provide care or to help a vulnerable person; and
- travelling to and from work, but only where this is absolutely necessary and cannot be done from home.

That's all – these are the only reasons you should leave your home.

You should not be meeting friends. If your friends ask you to meet, you should say No.

You should not be meeting family members who do not live in your home.

You should not be going shopping except for essentials like food and medicine – and you should do this as little as you can. And use food delivery services where you can.

If you don't follow the rules the police will have the powers to enforce them, including through fines and dispersing gatherings.

Figure 1: Boris Johnson announces lockdown

Poverty in (and because of) the pandemic

At the start of lockdown, Sarah explained the difficulty of just getting by:

> All our wages go on our bills and food – don't really have any spare especially since a lot of my extra duties [work] has stopped due to covid. I know I am lucky but it's hard at the minute – boys need bits for school, paper etc and would like to get some more reading books but prices have rocketed because everyone is at home. Just have to manage as spending more on food.

When the pandemic arrived in the UK, some of the Covid Realities participants faced new and immediate financial hardship, while others, already in poverty, faced the challenge of surviving in new and often terrifying circumstances.

For Georgie, a single parent of two young children, in receipt of Universal Credit, the pandemic undermined her efforts to build up a business (and escape benefits):

> I'm a single mum of two young kids and on full UC [Universal Credit]. I was running a small independent business, unpaid as we are in process of applying for CIC [Community Interest Company] status. Due to Covid-19 not only have we lost all our customers and therefore our potential to grow as a business and so work towards getting free from benefits.

For Lexie, the arrival of COVID-19 meant the loss of her husband's job and the new experience of claiming benefits:

> My husband lost his job due to Covid, which was horrific, stressful and beyond heartbreaking. That left us needing to apply for benefit help, which left us with no money for weeks, which obviously resulted in debt (debt is something I don't normally do, I was raised if you can't afford something you save until you can) so the impact on all of our mental health has been major.

But for many other Covid Realities participants, already in poverty before the pandemic began, the arrival of COVID-19 simply meant new pressures and new fears. Meg is a disabled, single parent, with three children (two of whom are now adults):

> As a disabled lone parent with an underlying neurological condition and co-morbidities, I consider myself vulnerable to Covid-19 … I cannot queue at supermarkets due to extreme pain and fatigue, and because I am not on a 'list' I cannot prove I need assistance. I have had to spend more money overall by subscribing to shopping services when I cannot get a slot at the supermarket as I am not prepared

to break down. I cannot afford to get ill (not in a financial sense – a pastoral sense) as my 16-y-o has poor mental health at the moment and there is no one to look after him if I become ill or worse, end up in hospital. I do not go out unless I have to.

Meg, Lexie and Georgie reflect the diversity among Covid Realities participants.[5] Among the parents and carers we worked with are disabled people who cannot currently work, families who lost work in the pandemic and those who faced financial hardship because of sudden and traumatic life events, such as the death of a partner. We also spoke with refugees and those seeking asylum, some of whom faced extreme hardship where they were classed as having no recourse to public funds (see Chapter 2). There were also parents and carers in paid work, but struggling with poverty all the same – families whose experiences show the hole in the 'work is the best route out of poverty' mantra. This diversity of experiences reflects the diversity of low-income households, and the varying factors that push people into poverty.

The collision of pre-existing poverty with the additional pressures and challenges of COVID-19 was often disastrous for families living on a low income. COVID-19 saw outgoings rise with children at home all day, while income remained the same or, for some, decreased, and normal sources of support – family, friends, after-school clubs – suddenly became unavailable.

Before the pandemic, families living in poverty routinely faced the insecurity that comes with struggling to get by on too little, trying to find ways to make a too-limited budget last the day, week or month. As a home-schooling single mother, Dot had struggled to balance the bills for years:

> I've home schooled my youngest for 2 years now …
> It's been lonely sometimes but I'm resourceful so
> it's not all been bad. Definitely financially draining.

But, with the arrival of COVID-19, these insecurities suddenly had to sit alongside wider insecurities about the pandemic: would your frail family member get ill? Would the prices in the shop continue to rise, making budgeting even more fraught with anxiety? Often, circumstances created by the pandemic – for example, home schooling – were inevitably harder (and more insecure) for families living in poverty. Sarah summarised the many pressures she felt from her multiple new lockdown roles:

> There is so much pressure on parents, I am really feeling that at the moment I am a mum, an employee, a cleaner, a cook, a teacher with zero time for me. I bet a lot of people feel like me.

All parents and carers faced uncertainties as their children were suddenly at home all of the time, but those living in poverty faced additional anxieties about how they'd feed their children, now that they could no longer rely on them getting at least one hot meal a day at school. Families living on a low income had to navigate increased financial, emotional and health insecurities because of the pandemic.

Sadly, and despite this, the government response completely neglected to provide targeted support for families with dependent children. The only support offered was temporary, and unavailable to some families. The most significant help provided was the £20 weekly increase to Universal Credit and Working Tax Credits, a large boost in benefit levels, but one offered only temporarily and not provided at all to those on legacy benefits,[6] including millions of disabled people and carers (social security is discussed in detail in Chapter 6).

'The basic range is not always there': managing disrupted budgeting practices

People on the lowest incomes are often experts at budgeting, deploying imaginative and time-intensive approaches to make their money stretch and last as long as possible. With the arrival of COVID-19, the pre-pandemic budgeting strategies that families on a low income relied upon suddenly became inaccessible, impractical or both. Shopping around in multiple supermarkets for reduced items and the cheapest prices was no longer an option, due to lockdown regulations. People were often forced to change where or how they shopped, which led to higher costs. Dorothy, a single parent to two children, explained:

> I have to do my shopping in small local shops so I can lock my children in the car and watch them. The butchers and petrol station does not have a massive variety – prices are a lot higher and smaller quantities so our budget which was over-stretched before is not even enough to last a week.

Accessing reasonably priced food was difficult, especially due to food shortages in the first few months. Georgie set out how her usual budgeting had to change:

> With the shopping because the announcements in Tesco's are saying 'shop for only what you need, get only what you need' you're under stress straight away to just grab what you need off the shelf. What I found today is that the basic range is not always there, there are lots of empty spaces on the shelf so you have to grab what there is and some of those products you wouldn't usually buy because, for me, it is usually a financial cost. I wouldn't normally go for branded products because that soon escalates in cost.

Trying to find time for the work of getting by alongside the new demands of home schooling was exhausting, with parents frequently also juggling fear and uncertainty around employment and related support.

Low-paid jobs and the pandemic: ongoing insecurity

On 20 March 2020, the government announced the Coronavirus Job Retention Scheme (JRS) – which widely became known as the 'furlough scheme'. Its purpose was to provide grants to employers to ensure that they could retain and continue to pay staff, despite the effects of the COVID-19 pandemic. Under the scheme, employers could furlough employees and claim a grant from Her Majesty's Revenue and Customs (HMRC) for 80% of their salary (up to £2,500 per month). Initially, it was intended to run only between 1 March 2020 and 31 May 2020, but was extended at least five times until September 2021. The furlough scheme clearly brought significant benefits, but because it only paid 80% of a worker's salary the Trades Union Congress (TUC) highlighted that this would mean many low-paid workers were actually being paid less than the national minimum wage.[7]

Levels of insecurity for people in precarious jobs added yet another layer of difficulty for families living on low incomes. Ironically, many of those in the most insecure and lowest-paid jobs were those suddenly classified as 'key workers', doing the essential work of keeping the country going at a time of crisis and being celebrated with warm words, if not living wages.

At the start of the pandemic, low-paid key workers had their hard work acknowledged with a weekly 'clap for carers'. We became used to Thursday night clapping for the National Health Service (NHS), local councils cutting 'thank you NHS' into grass verges and drawings of rainbows stuck in windows. For some parents this was an important expression of solidarity. As Sarah told us:

> We always look forward to clapping on Thursday so I think it's our favourite day. Boys love it as they are downstairs as well a bit later. Makes me feel proud of where I live and the community spirit, someone a bit further down even did a song after the clap tonight, which was lovely. Feel on a Thursday that everything is ok and we could keep going like this.

As welcome as this gesture was, however, it did little to address the systemic problems with a labour market that fails to reward low-paid but essential work such as the work of carers, of keeping our supermarkets stocked and of caring for our children.

People in insecure and low-paid work were especially at risk during the pandemic. The Joseph Rowntree Foundation, a charity which conducts and funds research aimed at solving poverty in the UK, reported[8] that people on zero-hours or temporary contracts were four times more likely to lose their job during the pandemic, and self-employed people were three times more likely to stop working, as compared to people on permanent contracts. The lowest-paid workers and part-time workers were twice as likely to lose their jobs, as compared to the highest-paid. A combination of this insecurity, coupled with having to access the social security system for the first time, impacted upon Polly, a furloughed mother of three children, and her family – changing their family dynamics and their sense of security:

> My husband got paid for last week today, his first wages in over 4 weeks. As someone who has always worked, he's really hated not earning money, having to depend on Universal Credit and my furlough pay, all of which goes into my bank account. It's been really hard for him asking me for money. It's also been hard for me having to budget with limited income.

Melissa was also struggling. A mother of two children, living on savings and furlough pay, she told us that although furlough was really beneficial, the extra insecurity and uncertainty that came with it was difficult to manage. The repeated, rolling, unpredictable extensions of the programme left families deeply insecure, not knowing for how long they could rely on this support:

> For us, like most people, it's been a combination of financial and practical worries. I know we are lucky as we have managed to get by on our savings and furlough, but the uncertainty is taking its toll a bit. We have made an effort to reduce our outgoings such as switching gas and electricity supplier, shopping at the best times of day for discounted food, not spending on any non-essential items and growing our own vegetables in our garden.

The insecurity of furlough, then, was clear – affecting families' behaviour, sense of security and their ability to plan.

Some groups are at heightened risk of being in insecure work. A major report from national charity for single parents

Gingerbread and a leading independent centre for research and evidence-based consultancy, the Institute of Employment Studies, found that single parents were twice as likely to have a zero-hours contract as other family types, putting them at greater risk of COVID-19 job insecurity.[9] Only 21% of single parents reported being able to work from home, compared to 38% of coupled parents. We saw these difficulties in the parents we were working with, too. Danni, a key worker with two children, told us:

> As a nurse and a single Mum it has been a difficult summer. Obviously I had to be at work, no chance of furlough or to work from home. My kids had to go to the hub school, which was a real godsend for me. There were days that they didn't like it but on the whole they enjoyed it. For me it was strange to drop my kids at a building I wasn't allowed into, with staff I didn't know, knowing my children had a new peer group that I will never meet or know the parents/ carers of. There was no real 'holiday' as we couldn't really go anywhere – except for the supermarket!!

There are clear gendered aspects here that were worsened by the pandemic – the majority of single parents are women (as were 70% of the parents who took part in Covid Realities), and they bear the brunt of juggling childcare, work and caring responsibilities.

Fears of COVID-19: 'a permanent feeling of unease'

Alongside managing daily budgets, insecure employment and navigating changes to the social security system, families on a low income also had to contend with significant fears around becoming ill with COVID-19, and what this might mean for their capacity to get by.

Uncertainty and constant anxiety were recurring themes in diary entries. The greatest fear single parents often faced centred on what might happen to their children if they caught the virus. The fear felt by Victoria – who had fled her abusive ex-partner, and remained terrified of being found by him – was palpable in her description of what would happen to her children, should she catch COVID-19 and die:

> I also learnt this weekend that if I catch the virus and die, or heck die of any cause really, then my kids would 'most likely be sent to their father' (even if I've written a will begging for my children's safety). To the man who threw my baby across a 13/14 ft room cos she was crying and he was watching TV. The man who'd hit my daughter anytime she spoke without permission or dared to say 'no' to an order. Who made both my kids sit still and silent for hours on a cushion on the floor just so he could dominate them and punish me for making him a cold brew or burning lunch. If I die my kids go to him? I'm horrified. I have no idea when I'll die but the way my body feels I have no trust in it to have many miles left.

Transmission – the risk of infecting others – also presented a major concern. When my next-door neighbour became ill with COVID-19 in April 2020, I spent ages asking Google 'Can coronavirus transmit through walls?' as I was so terrified of getting it. We can see how these anxieties around contracting COVID and passing it on to loved ones were a constant for participants. Connie, who has three children and worked part time while receiving Universal Credit, wrote:

> Another day and it feels the same. I am carrying a permanent feeling of unease. I can't put my finger on what specifically it is that is causing it but I'm gonna generalise and assume it's the current situation. Rationally thinking, not much is different for us. We don't miss the cinemas, shops, pubs and restaurants. I miss the frequency of seeing my friends and family. I haven't seen my grandad since July when we sat in his garden. I haven't hugged him since December last year. I worry that he'll die before we get to see him. I've now started to worry about what if something happens to me and the children find me

dead in bed or something. I'm not even unwell or have any underlying health conditions but this is an unwelcome thought that has crept into my mind.

Like Connie and so many of us, I remember feeling sick with worry, convinced that my then 93-year-old Gran would get ill before I had the chance to visit her again. When support bubbles (a support network that linked two households) were allowed in England and Northern Ireland from 13 June 2020, I was so worried about visiting Mam that I insisted she left sanitising wipes in the bathroom so I could clean everything down after I'd used it. That night, I remember sitting on her sofa with my heart pounding out of my chest, terrified that I would somehow infect her with COVID-19 and it would be my fault. Dorothy experienced similar worries:

> My son needs 24/7 care and attention. And as a single parent that's an awful lot so I'm allowed to mix outside my bubble for extra help or respite which I really do need. I go to my mum's most days or they come to my house. But that also leaves me an awful worry and paranoia all the time that if I was to pass on covid to my mum or dad and they were to get sick and anything was to happen to them and that it would be my fault and I would have to live with that and also that my family could hold me responsible for making them sick. So you can't win – it's a no-win situation for anybody.

Fears over family members' health meant that the pandemic led to loneliness and isolation for some people. Enzo, a single parent and caregiver, said:

> I'm finding it quiet, lonely and a little stressful when my daughter is at school as can't do anything else and there's nowhere to go as everywhere is shut and my mother is shielding and there's been a few Covid cases at the school so can't go near my mother just in case coz don't want her getting it.

For Charlotte, her main fear wasn't her parents catching COVID – it was that the isolation that was meant to protect them would damage their mental health irretrievably:

> My daddy has Covid. He is 62. Last year I nearly lost him in a horrific motorbike accident when he was at the Isle of Man TT. He recently told me 'It's not Covid that will kill me, it will be loneliness and depression and the fact I can't see my family.' This greatly concerns me. Loneliness and depression seem to be the 2 main mental health issues arising from Covid. It's tragic.

At the time of writing, the Office for National Statistics has shown that levels of loneliness in Great Britain have increased since spring 2020.[10] Areas with higher rates of unemployment tended to have higher rates of loneliness during the study period (October 2020 to February 2021).

Fear of catching COVID-19, as well as the costs of accidentally breaking lockdown rules, meant that some people were wary of leaving the house. Victoria's account below shows how some people maintained the vigilance and fear of the first lockdown, even when the lockdown itself had ended:

> Honestly, I'm acting like the first lockdown is still in place. Much easier for me that way, I'm terrified of catching the virus as I'm not confident in my chances if I caught it. As such, sod what stupid rules government puts out (which I do read up on and listen to and, quite often, roll my eyes at), I'm staying put and keeping myself and my family safe. I have no trust in the current leaders, I think they care only for their pockets and their reputation, not for the actual people of Britain. That said, the fines scare me. Money is so tight as it is I worry that I might accidentally break a rule and be fined. I can't afford to pay any fines, much easier and less stressful to just stay home and pretend the first lockdown is still on.

Fragmentation and failings of support

Lockdowns immediately and completely curtailed the possibilities of family and friends providing everyday support. This sudden withdrawal of informal support caused significant problems for parents and carers living on a low income, who often rely on the help and care of friends, neighbours and non-resident family members, as Dorothy describes:

> We spend so much more on electricity, food, gas as we are at home most of the time. We used to have lunch or dinner at my mum's after I got the children from school. Mum always picked up little things for us when she does her shopping, like washing powder or sweets or toys. Now we no longer can visit.

As we saw earlier, in announcing the first lockdown Boris Johnson stated: "You should not be meeting friends. If your friends ask you to meet, you should say 'No'. You should not be meeting family members who do not live in your home." This had a very real effect on families, who often had to seek out additional sources of support, such as charitable assistance from a food bank. Often, these services were unable to replace the gap left by lost family support, were inadequate to meet families' needs and increased feelings of stigma and shame.

Food bank use

Charitable support from food banks has skyrocketed since the pandemic began. The latest data[11] from the Independent Food Aid Network, a network for unaffiliated food aid providers, showed a 190% rise in the number of three-day emergency food parcels distributed by 83 independent food banks from May 2020 to May 2021. Children and households with children have long been more likely to require the additional charitable support that food banks can provide. Despite the fact that families with children aged 0–16 make up just 20% of the UK population, 39% of Trussell Trust food parcels went to such families across 2020/21.

Families felt let down and neglected by a government that seemed uninterested in and unaware of the needs of households living in poverty. They were consequently often reliant on and immensely thankful for food charity, as Erik, a single dad of one receiving Personal Independence Payments (PIP) and Disability Living Allowance (DLA), told us:

> Since shortly after the first lockdown started we have been receiving help from a local food bank with weekly food parcels which we could not have managed without and are extremely grateful for. We are only obtaining this help as my daughter attends [a] young carers [support group] and told them that I was struggling to buy food due to a lack of money and finding it hard to leave home due to a fear of catching Covid-19 and being unable to care for her as I have no real help or support from family or friends.

Parents and carers described having access to a food bank as a 'lifeline', but it also brought with it feelings of stigma, shame and guilt.[12] Alex felt the stigma of food aid acutely. For her, every trip to the food bank was a reminder of deep-rooted, gendered social injustice:

> I am aware of food banks. I walk to them and feel the humiliation knowing the father of my child is living in luxury as a businessman taking his pick from takeaway menus or eating out to help out.

Not only was it stigmatising to have to ask for food aid, but also the support on offer was often entirely inappropriate. Alex was offered seed potatoes that, without the luxury of a garden, she could not grow:

> Foodbank/larder has a new scheme. They are providing seed potatoes to plant to grow your own in your garden. I don't have a garden. Not sure if it's me just not organised or incapable but as a single parent caring for a SEN [special educational needs]

child full time, juggling bills, cleaning the flat and running up and down the road to the food bank has left me exhausted, never mind become a farmer.

Food that was offered was routinely inadequate to meet people's needs and, in some cases, inedible. Charitable food aid deprives people of agency and choice; people must take what they are offered and make the best of it, rather than making their own decisions about what they and their family want to eat. Victoria experienced guilt and shame when receiving inedible food:

> It's emotionally difficult to think I've been reduced to asking for stale and mouldy bread. I feel guilty for needing to access such assistance, I feel guilty for binning some of the produce given (my logic being that food poisoning could weaken my kiddies' immune systems and make them more at risk of the virus, better to go without bread than to risk getting ill by it). And I feel shame. At that moment, I felt disgusted at myself. What kind of mother does it make me?

She told us about the difficulties of relying on the fare that she was given – the too-salty tinned food, and the endless pasta with sauce:

> From this usual relief parcel we were given some biscuits, tinned beans and tinned meatballs and some 'add water' items. Of which we are grateful for but my kiddies are lately refusing to eat, saying they make them feel sick. They're sick of tinned goods. They miss me making meaty and healthy foods. My kids don't complain though, they never act spoilt over it, they don't turn their noses up ... when I offer [tinned meals] and will often join me to see what herbs or spices we have left to try and improve upon the meal options (I am very worried about our salt intake, especially kiddies, surely all these tinned salted goods aren't healthy!?) They try to eat but can

normally only manage a few mouthfuls before they say they can't stomach it no more.

Being reliant on charity left Victoria dreaming of meals of 'steak and greens', which felt an unobtainable luxury, rooted in choices she just didn't have. Some people, like Destiny, a single mother to one child, didn't seek help from a food bank even though they needed it because of worries over the perceptions attached to doing so:

> I always worry going to food banks would shine a negative light on my parenting skills. I'm on UC and I don't have a lot of money but I try to avoid getting help as I feel it would be admitting defeat.

For those who did use them, though, the cost in stigma and shame was often huge. Alex explains:

> I regularly use a foodbank or community larder as it's called. Lots of tins of spaghetti hoops and bread going out of date. Caters for milk intolerant and gluten free foods. Lots of knitted teddies, I've been offered but my daughter is 14. I feel the shame burning my cheeks every time I enter and leave the foodbank. The lady in charge is ultra jolly like a gameshow host constantly going live on social media.

Food banks and food aid charities can provide a partial fix that can assist people living in poverty *temporarily*, but ultimately, people continue to risk facing the chronic and multiple realities of poverty in the longer term because the underlying causes of food insecurity remain unaddressed.

As we've seen, charitable provision through food banks can also create new forms of stigma. People in poverty are often experiencing perpetual crises – vouchers for three days of tinned and pre-packaged goods from a food bank does little to address chronic poverty and insecurity. The Independent Food Aid Network (IFAN) in the UK has been a leading advocate for dignified, nutritionally adequate and culturally appropriate charitable food provision. IFAN argues that charitable food can *never* be a viable replacement for the money to purchase food in normal ways – in supermarkets, local grocers and in cafes. Through local-level partnerships, IFAN is pioneering a 'cash first' approach to food insecurity,[13] where people are provided with money to make their own choices rather than vouchers to access charitable food through a food bank, aligned to its broader call for a systemic approach to tackling poverty. The work of IFAN, like the experiences of Covid Realities participants, ultimately shows us that emergency food aid cannot and never will be the answer to the underlying problem of rising poverty and everyday hardship for millions of households. What is needed, then, is institutional support at a national level, through a social security system that protects people from poverty. Offering temporary grants that can't be relied on, or measures that are time limited, does little to relieve people of the daily struggles of getting by on a low income.

'Getting out': thinking about the future on a low income

The end of lockdown and the 'future' beyond that was, for many parents and carers, highly uncertain. For parents in work, as well as those looking for new work, the future of their employment was unclear and seemed out of their control. Right at the start of lockdown Polly, a parent of three children, described how the impact of continued social distancing on her high street retail job was worrying her:

> I'm worried about my job. The high street isn't going to be the same. Even if my shop reopens, it may end up shutting if it doesn't make enough money. We are used to long queues at the till, not possible if only a few customers are allowed in at once. We are worried that so many people will be unemployed, it will be very hard to get any work.

Sabira, a single parent receiving Jobseeker's Allowance, also described the uncertainty over being able to find employment at a time when few firms were recruiting. As a migrant from Pakistan, Sabira needed her employer to commit to sponsoring her work visa, which created a further obstacle to finding employment:

> I need to work, when and where? Hopes are there that once Covid-19 is over there will be lots of jobs but this hope is not that high.

For many families in poverty, the experience of lockdown was stressful and challenging on a low and often inadequate budget. In summer 2020, as the first lockdown came to an end, families worried how their futures would contrast to those of families with higher incomes, as people started to be able to enjoy greater freedoms. Holly explains:

> Moving forward, I wonder what the 'new normal' will be. Many families will be looking forward to a day at the seaside when they reopen. I wonder if we will be able to go. We don't have a car, so will a family of 5 be able to get seats on the bus now only 25% of seats are available? We don't have passports, we've never been on a plane, our holidays have been 4 nights at a Haven resort, something we've paid for in instalments. Now those who would normally go abroad can't, our holiday will be unaffordable. We weren't able to go this year anyway. But the prices are already double what they were last August.

What happened next? Beyond lockdown one

The pandemic affected us all, and brought additional layers of insecurity into all of our lives. The uncertainty, anxiety, fear and upheaval of the arrival of coronavirus in the UK will stay with us all for the rest of our lifetimes. None of us will ever forget having to wave at our family members through the window, checking daily death counts and being told to keep away from anyone who wasn't in our household. The mental health implications are already striking – we will see how this has affected Covid Realities participants in Chapter 5.

For families on a low income, life was made increasingly hard by the pandemic. Previous tried and tested strategies for managing already tight budgets, such as shopping around in several supermarkets and getting help from family and friends, were no longer possible. Food bank use jumped sharply, alongside wider increases in food insecurity overall – disproportionately impacting on families with children.

Fears around getting COVID-19 and keeping family safe were daily considerations that, again, have a profound, long-lasting impact that will last well into post-pandemic life. But, surprisingly, it hasn't all been negative – families did also tell us that they enjoyed spending more time with their children, which could lead to greater bonds (if the odd argument!). This tells us that the 'old normal' needs a rethink as we readjust to restrictions easing and the pressures of life become more intense.

We have seen how the combination of pre-existing poverty and the impact of the pandemic has caused devastating consequences for families on a low income that will likely have long-lasting effects. Political choices not to offer targeted support for those who needed it most reinforced the impact of these multiple, intersecting insecurities. This is a result of ideology rather than inevitability. Because of the absence of adequate, targeted support, families with dependent children living on a low income were left to navigate the storm of the pandemic on their own.

Lockdown and COVID-19 fears had to sit alongside the financial worry of finding money to put food on the table, to keep the house warm and to meet the cost of having the children home all the time. Despite all this, as summer appeared on the horizon, there were hopes that brighter days might be coming. But, as we were all about to find out, we were still very much at the beginning of the pandemic.

Chapter two
Summertime

Led by Jim

Summertime and the living is ...

Astronomically high. No money to go out for memory-making days, balancing food and bills always getting in the way.

Constantly living in a state of worry with no money to spare. Knowing I HAVE to be the one who worries, because no one else really cares. Everything is a necessity, needed here and now. Let's just add uniforms, shoes, coats, bags and stationery – watch those meagre finances swirl.

Desperate for the kids to go back to school, that should help ease household bills but not the guilt I feel. The dread of my kids going back is also real.

They have no fun tales to share. I wish I could enjoy my kids without fear, guilt and worry, so living in the summertime is not really fair.

Kim

Summertime and the living ...

ISN'T easy, the kids are jumping and the pollen is high. Your money's tight but your kids need an outing, so play little children, don't you cry.

Victoria

'The days I enjoy most'

As summer arrived and the days brightened, the national mood seemed to lift. Cases of COVID-19 had been falling steadily since their April 2020 peak, and on 23 June Boris Johnson announced an easing of the lockdown in England. After a devastating spring, attention turned cautiously toward the prospect of summer holidaymaking and the return of something like normal life. Beginning in early July, pubs, restaurants and hairdressers would reopen. For the first time in months, two households would be allowed to meet indoors. With this news, the national print and television media quickly began to focus on the easing of restrictions, the return of outdoor leisure and the possibility of regaining our social lives.

As we cautiously emerged to reunite with friends and family, it seemed that everyone was reeling, disoriented by what had happened – by what was *still* happening. At the same time the sense of emergency faded a little, leaving some space to reflect on what the crisis had revealed about the society in which we lived. As we saw in the Introduction, the idea that we are 'all in it together' often gets an airing during times of crisis, and this message certainly seemed to dominate the early months of the pandemic. But during the summer of 2020, social divisions and inequalities often seemed even more stark than they had before.

I[1] had mixed feelings about the easing of restrictions. On the one hand, I was desperate to get away and see my family, who lived more than 200 miles away. In March, when the first lockdown descended, my youngest daughter was only six months old and not yet crawling. Now, in July, she was ten months old, standing up and on the verge of walking. I was desperate for my family to meet her. And, to be honest, I was also looking forward to a bit of a break from non-stop parenting – a night out, or even better, a lie-in. On the other hand, I had little confidence that easing restrictions was the right decision. By turns dismayed and enraged by the mishandling of the pandemic response, I worried about the risks of unlocking, particularly for my parents, who are approaching old age. Like Kayleigh in the last chapter, I worried that in bringing their grandchildren to visit we might also unwittingly bring them the virus.

For Covid Realities participants too, the arrival of summer and the easing of restrictions brought mixed feelings. On the positive side, people wrote of their happiness at being able to leave the house for longer trips, making plans to visit friends and family. For Destiny, a single mum with a two-year-old, the change of weather alone brought with it new freedom:

> I am so grateful for the days with better weather as it opens up so much more things for us to do! We took a short drive to the Country Park and just having green space to let my kid run about and enjoy nature … it's just amazing. We left when it started to get too busy for me to feel comfortable but just the short time out in the sun in a beautiful area was just bliss.

When Destiny's family came to visit her from London, she 'hope[d] the days of running about parks continue as these are the days I enjoy most now'. The enjoyment of nature and being outdoors was a common theme in diary entries from the summer months. Meg described her pleasure at seeing 'bright pops of colour from the bedding plants all over the park as they were coming into their best bloom'. After months cooped up indoors, there was real delight that the easing of restrictions coincided with the arrival of brighter days.

As well as the pleasures of being outside again, there was joy in seeing friends and family – as there would be whenever subsequent lockdowns lifted. After the second lockdown, Lizzie, a single parent of two primary-school-age children, was excited by the prospect of renewing family contacts:

> I'm excited!!! I saw my Dad for the first time since November (door step visit on my birthday); last time we sat down together for a hug and chat was June last year. It meant so much for my daughters to spend time with Grandad. I'm looking forward to wandering round the shops, zoos, parks, theme parks, family days out. Having a drink in the pub with

friends or family. I have every hope that normality will resume and the lockdowns are over. Fingers crossed. Stay safe 🙏

Reading this entry, I'm reminded of mid-July, when we were finally able to take our kids to see their grandparents. After months of avoiding contact, I wasn't initially sure whether or not to give my mum and dad a hug. It sounds daft. It *felt* daft. But no such concerns troubled my eldest daughter, three at the time. Nothing was going to stop her from launching herself towards them, arms open. In Covid Realities entries, descriptions of similarly happy reunions also sit alongside entries recording the milestones and life events that couldn't be shared during the months of separation: births and birthdays, anniversaries and funerals. But more generally, in entries addressing summer, there was often the happiness of being able to see people again, and hope that the difficulties of lockdown might now be in the past.

Smokescreen

However, alongside the apparently simple and uncomplicated pleasures of being outdoors or reuniting with friends and family, there were also reservations about the relaxation of restrictions. Some of these reflected concerns about transmission, case rates and the government's ongoing mishandling of the COVID-19 pandemic. Throughout diary entries, it was apparent that most parents trusted the basic science, but held deep reservations about the political (and media) response. Danni, for example, told us:

> I don't trust the government at all. The media are often missing the point about what needs to be publicised and what doesn't.

Some people were also uncertain about whether they really wanted a return to normal life. In contrast with a media narrative that portrayed a public desperate to return to normal, some participants recalled the difficulties they had faced in 'normal' times, before the pandemic. Lockdown was overwhelmingly detrimental to people's mental health (as we'll see in Chapter 5), but some of the small respites it offered were real. This was not relief from poverty – as discussed in Chapter 1, and throughout this book, the pandemic and its restrictions imposed immense hardship on low-income families. Rather, the relief was from having to always undergo struggles and hardships in public view. Some participants worried that when public life resumed their feelings of guilt, shame and failure would only grow. As Gracie, a single mum and key worker in a school, wrote:

> COVID has actually given us a great smokescreen to hide income disparities behind – so if I couldn't have a day out, a cinema trip, a takeaway with friends, I can just use COVID as our excuse not to attend rather than the much more embarrassing truth: 'I can't afford it'. Often, even good friends, despite the well intended inspirational quotes posted all over their social media, get fed up with hearing you haven't got the money to do things, and COVID has really helped in that department.

The easing of restrictions, then, returned many families to the everyday run of difficulties and constraints they had experienced before the pandemic.

While the media narrative during that summer repeatedly returned to foreign travel restrictions and their impact on British holidaymakers, the most important restrictions faced by many Covid Realities participants had been there long before the pandemic. Reopening also brought new challenges. Chapter 1 described how the onset of lockdown severely disrupted many of the budgeting and shopping practices people had for getting by on low incomes. But when lockdowns lifted, things didn't simply return to normal. After disappearing during lockdown, some free or low-cost leisure options failed to make a return. Charlotte described how, while others enjoyed holidays, her children were unable to take any trips that summer:

> For the last few years a wonderful support group have been taking my 2 children on day trips to the beach,

parks, caves and indoor play areas. It's a free service which is funded. Due to Covid they were not able to take my children. I don't drive and I've very little money. My children didn't get a decent summer. They didn't get experiences they had got before. A simple day trip meant a lot to them. I feel bad for them. We don't have access to a caravan to escape. We don't have the money for hotels or a house in the country.

Not only were options for leisure and holidaymaking more limited than usual, they were also in higher demand. Nellie described how that summer, when things reopened, it was often with higher prices:

> So playgroups and soft play seem to be beginning to open up, which is great … if you have the money. All our free/low-cost playgroups are still closed. The toddler classes are open, but they're at least £5 a session! Our usual playgroup is going to open, and it's normally pretty reasonable at £2.50. But to make it Covid secure you have to book on for a 6 week term and pay upfront. And as for the soft plays. Because they can't have as many children in they've all hiked their prices. I saw one place charging £20 per table!

The free options were the first to close and the last to open. Playgrounds often remained padlocked, even as pubs and restaurants reopened.

The civic duty to consume

As the summer approaches, it is always common for small talk to turn to holiday plans, to hopes of getting to the beach, of days or weeks out with the children, of making memories. Summer 2020 had a less certain feel, but the need for a bit of a break and, even better, some time away, felt more essential than ever.

We know that families in poverty routinely struggle to afford holidays or even days out, with these being some of the first things to go when budgets are stretched almost unimaginably tight. In these new COVID times, parents in poverty needed a break as much as (if not more than) anyone, but – as ever – most often could simply not afford it. This left parents managing feelings of guilt and disappointment, for themselves and also for their children.

For Syeda, as for Gracie mentioned previously, the easing of restrictions brought with it new pressures rather than new freedoms, and this was something that left them both feeling out of step with the 'national mood':

> From today … we can go out and socialise more. Which as a benefit claimant simply means more cost. I know that sounds miserable, or ungrateful. But it cannot be avoided – it is going to cost me more now as the girls start going out with their friends.
>
> Even just this weekend my eldest daughter, legally visiting a school friend of hers and having a takeaway tea in her back garden, set me back an unexpected £10. It was all last minute so the extras from a meal I had frozen during the week, which I had defrosted for her, was wasted. Don't get me wrong, I loved the fact she was going out with her own friends after having had a dark winter, locked away alone, mostly in her bedroom.
>
> This shouldn't be a big thing – she should be making last minute plans and going out and enjoying herself. And she is – but I saw the cost of this first, before feeling happy she was going out … And then come the inevitable invites from friends to go out for a drink. Well, it won't be a drink, it will be a few. But for the price of a pint I could get 4 cans from the supermarket. Now I do know that sentence sounds miserable and ungrateful. Of course I want to see my friends and you cannot put a price on a laugh with your mates. But I will have to turn down several invites as I cannot afford it. I cannot tell them that, I just hope they don't see it as me being unsociable, or worse, unfriendly.

... The relaxing of the rules is what is going to
cause me problems. Little ones, but ones I need to
address somehow.

Subsidised and free provision such as holiday play schemes does
exist in places, but often there are financial barriers to accessing
this. For Aurora, even the free holiday-time provision provided
by her local council was unaffordable because of the costs of
getting there:

> Today I received a code from the council. They
> have provided a provision for summer clubs over the
> holidays. Whereas this is indeed a great step, we are
> still unable to make use of these due to the costs of
> travel to and from these places.

All this made for an uneasy and often uncomfortable emergence
from lockdown. Everywhere there were calls to get out, to enjoy
ourselves, to consume in cafes, in shops and in entertainment.
But this was not always possible for parents in poverty, who
often remained locked down by their financial hardship.

As part of his efforts to restart the economy, in August 2020
Chancellor Rishi Sunak introduced his notorious 'Eat Out to
Help Out' scheme, where consuming was recast as our civic
duty. Across August, from Monday to Wednesday, Britons
were invited to take their families out for a meal, with financial
incentives (the Treasury would pay half of the total bill, at a total
cost to the state of £849 million[2]).

Some parents in Covid Realities did make use of this scheme,
parents like Charlie:

> after the first lockdown I was helping at my local food
> bank and in August I was out and about a fair bit,
> taking advantage of the eat out help out [scheme].

But, for others, like Danni and Meg, they simply couldn't afford
to eat out, even with the government's support. Indeed, for
many families in poverty, eating out felt out of reach, which
then left them going without, but also often acutely aware of

how this set them apart from 'other' families. Alex described the impact this had on her:

> Lying in bed craving a plate of chilli. Facebook 'friends' raving about the new Taco Bell restaurant opened up in the city.
> New hair dos and nails done, got a tattoo.
> Am I missing something here? It's a pandemic and we as a nation are supposed to be all in this together. Oh yes they have husbands who work and share it with their family.

In Alex's account, we can sense the visceral hurt caused by her daily exclusion from the experiences that characterise life for so many. This is a central part of the harm that is done by poverty and inequality.

Sanctuary

The experiences of repeated lockdowns were at once universal and very particular to individual circumstances. When we are locked down in our houses, it matters more than ever what these places are like. It matters whether your house is habitable or not, and whether it provides access to outside green space (see Chapter 5). And it matters who you share your house with, as we saw with the increased risk of COVID infection for those living in multi-generational households, which regularly saw the mixing of working and elderly populations.

Chrissy had a tough start to the pandemic, having been hospitalised shortly before it began. In February 2020, while she was still recovering, her partner moved in with her, which was a huge source of support. This move, however, also led to several months of bureaucratic confusion as they tried to get their benefits sorted out to reflect their newly formed household. During this time, Chrissy was always thankful for her home

> on a post-war council housing estate, where a large number of houses are now private. It's very green and was designed that way. As one of the first houses

to be built, I have a larger-than-average garden, and
in my little bit of the estate, it's one of the smaller
gardens. I'm also fortunate to live 5 minutes from
large parkland, and beyond that there's open fields.
My garden is my sanctuary.

Being confined to our homes and localities during the pandemic
often prompted greater reflection on our relationship to
the spaces and places where we lived, and on their qualities
and problems. For some, like Chrissy, there was a renewed
appreciation for the sense of safety and security they felt at
home. For others, lockdowns intensified existing feelings of
alienation, disconnection or insecurity.

Individuals experiencing domestic violence were at elevated
risk in lockdowns, especially where they were locked down with
the perpetrator of abuse. Indeed, when the first lockdown was
announced there was widespread alarm among domestic abuse
campaigners about the impact this would have. There were
fears that abuse would increase, and that victims would find it
only harder to access support. These fears were well grounded.
A year into the pandemic, the charity Refuge, which supports
victims of domestic abuse, shared evidence that showed a rapid
increase in calls to their National Domestic Abuse Helpline
since the first lockdowns were announced. Commenting on
this rise, the charity said:

> home is not a safe place. Lockdown measures,
> where women have been isolated and confined
> with their perpetrators more than ever before, have
> compounded their exposure to violence and abuse.[3]

Among the Covid Realities participants, several are survivors of
domestic violence. In the main, they had left abusive partners
before the pandemic began, but the experience of previous
abuse heavily shaped their experiences of the lockdowns in very
particular ways.

Danni explained the impact it had on her when she had to
rely on her abusive ex-partner for childcare to enable her to
stay in work:

I lost 2 childminders due to the pandemic and I've had to rely on my unreliable domestically abusive ex to look after the children more. It is not a comfortable place to have to rely on your abuser so you can work ... And now he has decided to make a claim against me through the CMS [Child Maintenance Service], he owes me a lot through the CMS but it's a new claim so is assessed separately, again a government system that sucks.

Lockdown could also bring back disturbing memories. Meg is a divorced mum of three children. Her ex-partner had been controlling and coercive, and the controls of lockdown provoked memories that were sometimes difficult to handle:

Old memories of being domestically abused have resurfaced – particularly that of control & coercion. My son's Dad would lock me in the house to prevent me from leaving when I felt under threat from him. Although I didn't go out much before lockdown due to disability, at least I could choose when & where I could go. Now it is proscribed & I'm finding that aspect hard – it has definitely affected my mental health negatively, despite already taking long term antidepressants.

Meg was not the only participant to tell us that memories of gender-based violence were triggered by lockdown. This made already difficult circumstances even harder to manage. Like Meg, Alex had also been abused by her former partner. In her diary, she wrote:

I'm always on edge. I have dread in the pit of my stomach of what is going to happen next. Similar to how I felt when staying with my ex. He controlled the income and punished me for anything that was not my fault. The prime minister and his friends are the same. Controlling, greedy, self-serving.

The experience of domestic abuse places people at increased risk of poverty, particularly in situations where they are fleeing abuse.[4] Jasmine escaped domestic violence, and subsequently experienced significant hardship:

> I decided to put my situation in words. I am 33 yrs old. My daughter is 13 yrs old. Am single mum. Who escaped domestic violence from my own family few years ago. I raise my daughter alone. I can honestly say the guilt I feel inside is something I can't explain. I can't afford internet so my child has not done homework. She has basically been that bored my child has become self destruct[ive]. I currently have no cooker. Council has refused me. I live on £543 a month. And basically get no support.

Jasmine claimed Universal Credit and lived in what can only be described as destitution.

Having survived domestic abuse, many participants told us that their experience of the benefits system did little to support them. It was common for women with experience of abusive and violent relationships to draw direct parallels with their experience of the benefit system. Just as they felt they had to shoulder the blame for choosing a 'bad' partner, so they were made to feel culpable when they left an abusive relationship and turned to the social security system for support.

Victoria explains how she experienced fear and anxiety when she received communications about her Universal Credit claim:

> I'm really hoping this is an overreaction of anxiety on my part. In my mind I often have panic attacks on universal credit where things happen that mirror how my ex would treat me, so it's possible my anxiety is blown out of proportion here because of my experiences with my ex (such as anytime my ex said we needed to talk, me or my kids would get hurt, so I'm pretty fearful of what it means when people say they need to talk to me).

The social security system should be a place of refuge, even sanctuary, for people fleeing domestic abuse, but too often its inadequacy and its punitive design and delivery mean it is the opposite of that.

'A massive kick in the teeth': a key worker's experience

People's experiences of the pandemic were also greatly affected by whether they were in work or not, and if in paid employment, the kind of work they were doing. Gracie, whom we met earlier, was a key worker in a school and worked throughout the pandemic (although closed for many children, schools remained open for vulnerable children and the children of key workers). As a single parent, this was an enormous challenge that left her feeling overburdened and full of guilt:

> Being a single parent, lockdown has been tough. As a key worker I have worked throughout and my daughter was home alone all week when schools weren't fully open. She could have had a key worker space but I couldn't get her there as the school days were shorter and I was too scared to let her get 2 buses each way ... So my daughter was alone, dealing with rubbish internet, an ancient laptop – for months. It was awful. My job has been hugely stressful and I just have felt so, so guilty. I haven't been here for her in any sense of the word, yet I have been bending over backwards to support other families for my job. It's abhorrent. My friends seem to have forgotten we exist and my family is full of medical issues meaning we haven't seen them. Sometimes I cry and think I won't stop. But I have to pretend everything is fine for my daughter. But I don't think I'm very good at that.

The shutdown of Gracie's normal support networks – a nearby school, friends and family – made the routine juggling that goes along with being a single parent almost impossible, and she suffered as a result. She paid the price of working through the pandemic in guilt and stress and tears. This was a price that

– Gracie felt – went unrecognised. Worse than unrecognised, she felt her efforts were doubted. Like other school workers, Gracie risked her health on a daily basis, working indoors with other people, so that schools could remain open. In doing so, she performed a vital public service, since it meant that other key workers were able to continue working. As evidence mounted about the higher rates of infection and death among key workers – school workers among them – teaching unions demanded greater clarity on plans for the wider reopening of schools, and that their workers be given adequate personal protective equipment (PPE). One strand of the political and media response to this was to portray teachers as lazy and work-shy. In June 2020 the head teacher of a school in Sunderland was suspended by the school's governors and placed under investigation after saying, during a BBC Radio Newcastle appearance, that some teachers were using the pandemic as an excuse to 'sit at home doing nothing', adding that 'lots of HR rules, regulations, unions and people can say all reasons why they can and can't work'.[5]

The story was enthusiastically picked up in the press, from the *Daily Mail*, the *Telegraph* and the *Sun* to the *Daily Mirror*. The use of COVID-19 precautions as an excuse to avoid work became a popular theme, especially in right-leaning and lockdown-sceptical publications, with teachers often being singled out. In August 2020 the *Sun* columnist Dan Wootton wrote that 'Coronavirus is now being used as an excuse not to provide anything slightly difficult or complicated in all areas of our lives. But when it comes to education, the costs of that lazy caution are too great.'[6] 'It has been intensely stressful,' Gracie wrote. 'Working in a germ filled school, while simultaneously being told we school staff are lazy and selfish.'

Not only did Gracie feel her efforts were doubted, but also the material hardships she already faced as a low-paid worker were further exacerbated during the pandemic. Later on in the year, during winter, long after 'Clap for Carers' had ended, Gracie's fridge broke:

> [B]ut the charity shops were shut – so I had to do without – luckily this was through the winter so

I kept some stuff outside in a sealed plastic box to keep it cold.

Also in the winter, while self-isolating after having contact with a positive COVID case, she ran out of credit on the gas meter and 'just had to put extra layers on and sit with a blanket on my lap while working'.

That Gracie struggled financially while working is not unusual. Just before the pandemic, rates of in-work poverty[7] in the UK hit a high of 17% of working households – more than one in six. Among the worst affected were households with single earners, but increasingly households with two incomes (one full time, one part time) were being drawn into poverty.[8] There are a number of reasons for this – spiralling housing costs, inadequate social security – among which are the diminishing returns from work itself. Since the Great Financial Crisis of 2007–08, wages in the UK have not only stagnated but fallen in real terms.[9]

When, in November 2020, Chancellor Rishi Sunak announced a public sector pay freeze affecting Gracie, it hit her hard:

> Found out today my pay will be frozen again for 3 yrs – we only just had a 10 yr pay freeze. Here we go again. Working a million hours a day throughout lockdown and now I have to pay for the furlough scheme. Thankful to have a job obvs, but it is a massive kick in the teeth.

Gracie was one of several parents taking part in Covid Realities who worked in either education, health or childcare settings, and struggled to get by. This vital caring work remains undervalued and underpaid, with reports that many nursery workers are leaving the sector because they simply cannot afford to stay.[10] This is symptomatic of wider problems with our social and economic structures, and a more general reluctance to properly invest in and enable care work (both paid and unpaid).

Helen was a childminder, balancing the care of her child with the care of other people's children. The combination of her self-employed income and Universal Credit was not enough to lift her out of poverty, making every day a struggle:

> Today as I sit and prepare for our first full week of home schooling alongside me being a registered childminder the feeling of dread looms high. I have £6 in my electric meter, I have £0 money to top it up, I have no coal for the fire and I'm burning my home heating oil to keep us warm, a source I try not to use all day because I can't just buy £20 of oil ... I don't drink I don't smoke I don't have a fancy house or car, I haven't bought anything new in over a year. I prioritise my child and now I can't even buy her clothes when she has barely anything to wear ... Children do not deserve this, they don't need to know we are penny pinching, they shouldn't be cold or hungry especially now they are at home more and they still have to learn.

Helen, like Gracie, was at the sharp end of in-work poverty, struggling to get by, and with her paid care work poorly remunerated.

It is very common to hear politicians draw moralistic distinctions between people in and out of work. This neat (and overly simplistic) division has a very long history, but was ratcheted up during the Cameron and Osborne years with their rhetoric of 'strivers and skivers' (see Introduction). The ideological work of this rhetoric creates the space that allowed our former Chancellor, Rishi Sunak, to announce help with the cost-of-living crisis for 'working families' in the October 2021 Budget. It goes unsaid, but the suggestion is that non-working families do not need – or perhaps deserve – this help.

We're all used to hearing politicians 'big up' the virtues of working. But it is much less common to hear politicians talk about the very different experiences that people have of work; about widening inequalities in pay and conditions – excessive pay and low pay; or about the precarious insecurity of a life strung together across a succession of zero-hours and fixed-term contracts. The distinction between employers who pay a real living wage and those who do not receives much less scrutiny, and is not presented in the same moral terms as distinctions between so-called 'hard-working citizens' and everyone else. In the wake of Brexit, Boris Johnson's government set out an agenda to 'level up' the UK by creating a high-wage, high-productivity economy. Yet precisely how the government intends to tackle issues of job quality and low wages remains unclear.

And if politicians seem reluctant to talk about experiences of paid work, they appear even less keen to acknowledge the value and significance of the various unpaid forms of work that people do as parents and carers, the burden of which disproportionately falls on women. The singular and determined emphasis on 'hard-working families' excludes not only those who cannot work, or cannot find work, but also people who choose parenting and caring over paid employment. The social security system provides little scope for people to care for others – unless, as in the case of Helen and Gracie, it is as a form of paid employment. More often than not, such work is low paid and places significant pressure on other people, like family members who are dependent on the care of these workers. As a result, people like Gracie felt as if they were 'bending over backwards' for others – only to be rewarded with a 'kick in the teeth'.

Setting out the debate about employment and social security in terms of 'strivers and skivers' has proven a very useful way to avoid dwelling on inequality and exploitation in contemporary Britain. But during lockdowns, such injustices were starkly exposed, finding grim expression in statistics revealing different rates of infection, hospitalisation and death according to levels of social deprivation.[11] These uncomfortable facts gave the lie to claims that we were all in it together.

'The great leveller'

Lockdown and its restrictions had made life difficult in new ways, but for many Covid Realities participants, 'normal life' before the pandemic had not been easy either. This was something that the 'all in it together' rhetoric would attempt to obscure, but it was a truth that could not easily be hidden.

In April 2020, a clip from the BBC current affairs programme *Newsnight* went viral. It was a clip of the programme presenter, Emily Maitlis, opening the show, as was usual, with a direct address to camera. "They tell us coronavirus is a great leveller," she said. "It's not. It's much, much harder if you are poor." She went on:

> 'The language around COVID-19 has sometimes felt trite and misleading. You do not survive the illness through fortitude and strength of character, whatever the Prime Minister's colleagues will tell us. The disease is not a great leveller, the consequences of which everyone, rich or poor, suffers the same. This is a myth which needs debunking.'[12]

Maitlis appeared to be taking direct aim at government ministers, such as Cabinet Office minister Michael Gove who used the occasion of Prime Minister Boris Johnson's hospitalisation with COVID-19 to describe the virus as a 'great leveller'. Gove had earlier told a press conference, "[t]he fact that the prime minister and the health secretary have contracted the virus is a reminder that the virus does not discriminate".[13] With the Prime Minister in hospital, acting PM Dominic Raab had assured the public of his confidence that Johnson would "pull through" because "if there's one thing I know about this Prime Minister, he is a fighter".[14]

The myth that Maitlis was 'debunking' was that, when faced with the virus, we were all equals, facing equal risks. It was also the idea that beating the virus was a matter of personal strength, effort and willpower. For people living on low incomes, or dependent on income from the social security system, there might be something familiar about this 'myth', and its peculiar mix of contradictions. On the one hand, there is the idea that we all confront risk as equals – whether the risk of contracting a virus, or the various risks of social and economic life. On the other hand, there is the idea that the outcomes of our confrontations with such risks – success or failure – reveal pre-existing moral qualities that justify any inequalities that emerge.

Against the idea that coronavirus was a great leveller, or a measure of character, Maitlis spoke of the occupations most exposed to the virus, and of the workers most likely to fall ill: supermarket workers, bus drivers, care home workers – all among the lowest paid in our society. She also spoke of how lockdowns were tougher for people living in tower blocks and small flats, and for people in manual jobs unable to work from home. Maitlis ended her address by saying "this is a health issue with huge ramifications for social welfare, and it's a welfare issue with huge ramifications for public health".

What made this broadcast noteworthy and unexpected was not its content of relatively uncontroversial truths, but the fact that it was so rare to hear these things acknowledged and discussed, especially at that point during the pandemic.

Already used to being maligned by politicians and the media, many participants were already highly sceptical about such heavily underlined public narratives about a shared pandemic experience. They were also doubtful about the media's ability – or willingness – to hold the powerful to account. When we asked participants about their trust in government and the media, many people wrote to complain about both. Chrissy wrote, '[t]he media has failed to hold the Conservatives to account – investigative journalism is very thin on the ground. Cabinet aren't questioned or pulled up on their comments.' Rosie told us, 'I have never had much trust in the government to support families on low incomes. The pandemic has highlighted so many inequalities. It's clear the economy is their priority while ordinary people are struggling alone.'

The experiences of families on low incomes during the pandemic meant that they regarded narratives of national unity with a sceptical eye – but such narratives were often difficult to ignore.

Pandemic nation

The historian Benedict Anderson describes the nation as an 'imagined community' – imagined because no one can ever know or meet everyone in it, 'yet in the minds of each lives the image of their communion'.[15] When we think of ourselves as

UC
US
COVID
REALITIES
PEOPLE
Family
LEVEL UP
Children VOICE
ECONOMY
HOW
Better Life
Equality
communities
Caree
INCOME
WORK
JOBS
Potential
UPLift
Opportunities
EMpowerMent

belonging to a nation, we imagine ourselves alongside countless others whom we will never meet, but with whom we share our nationality.

During lockdown, unable to meet the people we *did* know, it was as if this national imagination went into overdrive. Watching the pandemic spread across the globe, we were invited to see ourselves, first and foremost, as members of a national community. On TV news bulletins we were shown graphs and charts comparing national infection rates, national case rates and national mortality rates like the scoreboards of a macabre international tournament. The phrase 'we are all in this together' invited us to imagine ourselves as members of the same national team.

For Anderson, the sense of modern nationhood arose with the printing press, and with the newspapers in whose pages readers could feel part not just of their own local community but of the nation as a whole. During the pandemic we turned not to printed pages but to the glowing screens of our smartphones, tablets and televisions. Our attentions were united around daily press briefings and prime ministerial announcements, and more loosely around a series of shared experiences: an encounter with empty supermarket shelves, or locked playground gates, shocking enough at first sight to document on smartphones and share via WhatsApp, Twitter or Instagram; poster-painted rainbows arching across the windows of each street. However, while for some the national narrative of struggling through the pandemic together might have been both plausible and a source of comfort, for others it only underlined their exclusion. When Howie woke up to the scandal surrounding free school meal replacements, she took to her diary to write:

> I have the red mist this morning! Discovering that some people have been able to save during this pandemic was a blow and a shock this week. But I am totally floored by the fact that some companies have been giving families only about £5 worth of food when they are allocated £30, meaning, like we all know deep down, that some companies have actually made a choice to profit from those struggling with

> poverty. It is utterly immoral. The idea that we are all
> in the same storm but with different boats just blew
> up for me this morning, we all know we don't have
> the same boats but actually some people/companies
> are not even in a storm at all, they are sunning it on
> a calm safe beach somewhere while we work out
> how to ride the coming tsunami with a rubber ring!

Out of the shared experiences of the pandemic, an attempt was made to craft a national narrative about being 'in it together'. Yet, as is often the case with such narratives, what is presented as shared and universal on closer inspection reveals itself to be much more partial, and involves the exclusion of ideas and experiences which don't easily fit.

These kind of national narratives are also partial in the sense that, by definition, they stop at the nation's borders.[16] Some of those who suffered most during the pandemic were people with the least secure claim to 'Britishness' (regardless of whether they were British or not) – people who were, in different ways, excluded from the national narrative of the pandemic.

'My British son'

A small number of Covid Realities participants were refugees, people seeking asylum or migrants with permission to live and work in the UK but with 'no recourse to public funds'. To have no recourse to public funds means that you are prevented from claiming social security benefits such as Universal Credit or Child Benefit,[17] as well as housing-related support (including for homelessness). As research by Citizens Advice[18] has shown, such people faced extraordinarily difficult conditions during the pandemic. Without entitlement to benefits, this left people with no choice but to work (if their residency status permitted this) or face destitution and homelessness. This is no accident, but the explicit intention of government policy: in 2012 the then British Home Secretary, Theresa May, announced a set of policies designed to make life unbearably difficult for undocumented migrants. In her own words, "The aim is to create, here in Britain, a really hostile environment for illegal [*sic*] immigrants."[19] As part of creating this hostile environment, access to public funds for those seeking asylum was stripped back even further. Without access to housing support, people seeking asylum have no choice about where they live. Without access to regular benefits, they must rely on cash support of only £39.63 a week.

Mindy lived with her two-year-old son in a single room of bed-and-breakfast (B&B) accommodation. As a 'Zambrano carer' with pre-settled status, she was not entitled to claim income-related benefits. She had no recourse to public funds, and experienced the harsh impact of this. For Mindy, the hostile environment was having its intended effect, and she did not feel welcome in the UK. Indeed, she felt actively excluded and ignored. As she explained:

> I didn't vote in the last election. I was finally eligible to do so after waiting ages for my pre-settlement status. I just couldn't bring myself to do it. No party cares or is talking about people who were left behind during COVID, specifically children like my British son, who through no fault of their own have one non-British parent like me. I'm a Zambrano carer. We are more often than not single women of colour and we are banned from accessing mainstream benefits to discourage benefits tourism. Not even child benefit. If my son lived with his British father then he would be entitled to state help, but because I'm his mother and he lives with me, I cannot claim any help. I got a job yesterday and after my calculations I realised it only leaves me £100 over after rent (in a 1 bedroom flat) and childcare for me to work. So I must buy food, pay council tax, transport, clothing, medicine and everything else on £100. We aren't even entitled to a council house or housing benefit to help. How is that not criminal? The alternative is continue living in one room in a 13 bedroom B&B with shared facilities with drug addicts and alcoholics and live off £74 a week. But even my social worker is warning support will be cut off soon and I must become self

sufficient soon. How? These British children are not all that British, are they?

Zambrano carers are people from non-EEA states[20] who are granted the right to live and work in the UK because they are the primary carer for a child (or dependent adult) who is British.[21] As a Zambrano carer, Mindy's right to live and work in the UK came from her role as her British son's only available carer. This 'Zambrano right' is named after the 2011 judgment of the Court of Justice of the European Union (CJEU) in the case of Ruiz Zambrano.[22] This case concerned a Colombian couple – Ruiz Zambrano and his wife – who had sought asylum in Belgium, were refused, but nonetheless couldn't be returned to Colombia because of the ongoing civil war. Remaining in Belgium, Ruiz Zambrano worked without permission (and paid social security contributions) while the couple tried to obtain legal permission to stay. In the meantime they had two children, who both acquired Belgian nationality and EU citizenship. The family were economically self-sufficient until it was discovered that Ruiz Zambrano had been working without permission, and he lost his job. When refused unemployment benefit because he didn't have permission to live or work in Belgium, Ruiz challenged the decision, and the case eventually made its way to the CJEU.

Ruiz Zambrano sought to derive a right to live and work in Belgium based on his children's EU citizenship. If the couple were unable to live and work in Belgium, they would be forced to leave, effectively denying their dependent children their citizenship rights. When the CJEU decided in Ruiz's favour, the UK government had to amend its own regulations to allow such 'Zambrano carers' to live and work in the UK too. This offered a route for non-EEA nationals to settle in the UK. In response, and as part of creating a hostile environment, the UK introduced amendments to social security legislation stripping such carers of their entitlement to non-contributory benefits, income-related benefits, Child Benefit and Tax Credits, and to housing benefit and homelessness assistance.[23]

As Mindy tells us, the impact of this hostile environment was profound insecurity for her and her son. Because Mindy is not a British citizen, her son is made to face increased hardship and difficulty by the denial of Child Benefit and housing support. In this way, Mindy and her son's belonging is placed in question: as she powerfully put it, '[t]hese British children are not all that British, are they?' This actively hostile policy, the hostile environment, left people like Mindy and her son particularly vulnerable during the pandemic and lockdowns. When summer arrived, and things began to reopen, people like Mindy and her son were able to enjoy going out and visiting parks like everybody else. But they did so carrying a heavy weight of financial hardship, a hardship that is a result of deliberate political decisions.

Beyond questions of nationality or immigration status, racially minoritised people more generally were disproportionately represented among COVID-19 deaths. This was due to higher rates of underlying health conditions, higher rates of social deprivation, and being more likely to work in the types of jobs most exposed to the virus.[24] The way that different factors – health, housing, deprivation, employment – intersect and together conspired to kill racially minoritised people at higher rates than White people is one example of structural racism: the accumulated impact of historical, institutional and cultural forms of racial discrimination. This was something that caused participants from racially minoritised backgrounds extra stress and worry. As Amber, a single parent working part time, told us:

> As for the future, I am wondering whether life will be back to normal. I wonder when I will feel ready to go out with my friends like we used to do. I have been filled with extra fear because of my ethnicity and I hope we all appreciate that we need to go back out there with extra caution.

Amber was worried because of higher mortality rates among minoritised ethnic groups. But on top of this, COVID-19 also brought with it heightened risks of suffering racist abuse and discrimination. An Independent SAGE[25] report in June 2020 noted how government and media communications sometimes increased the racism faced by minority ethnic and religious groups, with minority ethnic groups being routinely stereotyped and discriminated against because of perceived links with the disease.[26]

Hanging on

At the start of the pandemic, I lived with my family in a two-bedroom tenement flat in the Govanhill area of Glasgow. Our street, Victoria Road, was a grand Victorian boulevard leading in one direction to the city centre, and in the other to the wrought iron gates of Queen's Park. On the crossroads with Alison Street, our flat sat above a Greggs bakery, a pawnbrokers and a chaotically stocked gift shop called 'Happy Days'. Directly across the way from us was the Victoria Bar, a Celtic FC supporters pub. On match days you could follow the score by listening to the reactions from the crowd inside. Fridays were karaoke night, and someone always gave a rendition of 'Dirty Old Town'.

One day in summer, before the pubs reopened, I noticed a gathering of Victoria Bar regulars assembling outside in small groups, all two metres apart. A funeral cortege came down Alison Street and the masked mourners formed a line over Victoria Road, stopping the traffic, applauding as the coffin passed on its way.

I loved living in Govanhill, and on Victoria Road, although with first one and then two very young children the noise from the pub and from the traffic wasn't always ideal. As one of the most diverse and densely populated parts of Scotland, it was a well-known place that often elicited strong reactions. Often stigmatised by people who didn't live there, its residents the targets of racist abuse and intimidation, it was also a wonderfully warm community that welcomed people from very different places and walks of life – a sanctuary of sorts. Sometimes, during lockdown, living in such busy proximity to others was comforting, and a source of support and connection. When we all came down with COVID-19 as a family, our neighbours brought us groceries and treats. Hearing a knock one day during our isolation, I opened the front door to find a paper bag sitting on the step containing a tub of ice cream and four cones. We ate them with the windows open, gazing out at the street below.

But at other times, especially during the summer, I sometimes longed for something like suburban quiet, and doors that opened directly onto a patch of private outdoor space. On these days we would head out to Queen's Park and, if it wasn't raining, find somewhere to sit on the grass, letting our kids crawl and run about. On sunny days it would often seem that the whole of the Southside of Glasgow was in that park, together.

In Glasgow, through those lockdown months, I did feel a sense of solidarity, of community, of togetherness. This everyday togetherness stood in contrast to the garish, faux solidarity being manufactured by politicians and by much of the media, an artificial and jarring effort to unite, when so much was in fact divided and unequal.

In the national narrative, summer and unlocking was supposed to be a time of hope and liberation, but this wasn't always or even often the case for people living on low incomes. Against the false unity offered by national 'all in it together' narratives, this chapter has explored some (but by no means all) of the differences and inequalities underpinning people's experiences of the pandemic. As the Introduction set out, when COVID-19 arrived on its shores, Britain was a place suffering acutely from the dereliction – even destruction – of its public institutions and services. Growing inequalities were magnified still further by the pandemic. People also suffered from the effects of intersecting forms of disadvantages and discrimination, and for people whose position in society was already marked by oppression and injustice, summertime was often a matter of hanging on. The next chapter explores what happened when, after summer, the schools reopened and society continued its attempt to resume its normal seasonal schedule.

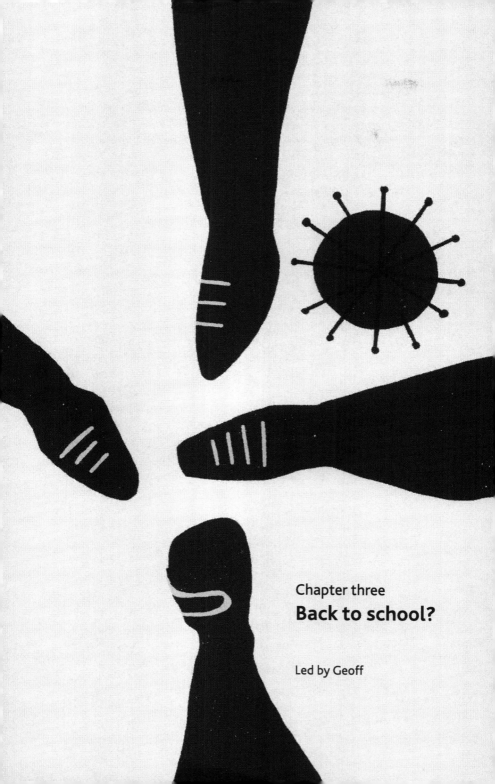

Chapter three
Back to school?

Led by Geoff

During lockdown my son's anxiety towards school doubled. Some nights the thought alone of going back and leaving our safe family bubble was too overwhelming and crippling for his little head to navigate around. It broke my heart the day my son (who is 7) looked at me with tears in his eyes and said 'mummy I don't want to be here anymore'. In that moment I knew he was broken and so far from the happy child he used to be.

Lola

Never again do I ever want to home school. As a qualified secondary school teacher I assumed I could do this. That I had this in the bag. No chance. It was literally the hardest thing I've ever tried to do. I have a very challenging 8 year old and he would just hit out and beat his 12 year old sister. We didn't have WiFi during the pandemic and the children's primary school had limited resources. I used the one encyclopaedia in my house as well as any reading books, and sometimes I would make up lessons to do with Volcanoes and Pompeii, the Lost City. Now, there's so much uncertainty about the return to school. My daughter is now in grammar school and she is worried about wearing a mask for the entire day. She also didn't get her final year in Primary School or the transitional experience moving from primary to secondary. I worry about children's mental health due to the lack of communication they have had with their friends and also from their lack of education. I look at my daughter, I see her worried face and her concerned look and the tears in her eyes. It's difficult for a mother to watch your child go through this.

Charlotte

Relief – 'K' has gone back feeling more positive – let's see how long that lasts. But 'R' has gone to uni. Back to school means we are financially much worse off. We had so much worry about school uniforms. Shoes. Uni stuff. I cried. I cried a lot.

Rosie

School in the pandemic has been a strange thing. As I[1] write, my six-year-old is behind me, self-isolating and so unable to attend school. We are lucky – safe, warm and fed – but this has not been the case for everyone. The handful of weeks leading up to the first school closures left a lasting impression. After the first UK cases were confirmed in January 2020 (coincidentally in a hotel above our local Co-op supermarket, 200 yards down the road), a simmering weirdness set in during the following weeks as it became clear that community transmission was beginning to escalate, and rapidly. The beginning of March was characterised by uncertainty at the school gates as awkward parents tried to hover an unknown distance from one another. How close can we stand? Who is infectious? What do infected people even look like? No rules yet, no set distances, no masks, and shops entirely out of alcohol-based hand gel. Just a lurking sense of impending dread, an unknown virus on the loose and a world on the brink of change.

My email 'sent' box tracks the strangeness as it develops. On Wednesday, 11 March, I was trying to arrange school drum lessons. By Monday, 16 March, along with 20–30% of other parents, I had pulled my son out of school. On Wednesday, 18 March, the Education Secretary announced that all schools in England would be closing as of the following Monday. A week later, as an asthmatic single parent, I made an appointment to write a will.

Schooling from this point took a wobbly path. There was chaos over exams, long months of home schooling, variable provision of substitutes for free school meals and flip-flopping messages about the (re-)opening of school for children of various ages. Throughout, schools stayed open for the children of key workers and for those in vulnerable families. Finally, though, schools returned for all pupils throughout August and September 2020.

In this chapter, we document how this played out. As in other areas, the guidance and government policy were often far from clear. There were some big gaps in provision, for example around free school meal replacements, with this gap only filled after the intervention of footballer-turned-campaigner Marcus Rashford. This chapter explores the perception among parents that their children formed a 'lost generation' – missing out on opportunities because of COVID, but also because of their disadvantaged starting point. In this sense, they felt multiply marginalised and all too often forgotten in the policy response. This was apparent from the very beginning of the pandemic. School closures and a shift to home schooling were implemented without any proper efforts to address the barriers to learning created by poverty (most notably, lack of access to the technology and wifi suddenly needed to take part in online lessons).

Free school meals: access and adequacy

This failure to support families in poverty with the fast-changing landscape was also apparent in what happened to free school meals, and efforts to replace them during periods of school closures.

The number of children receiving free school meals in England had soared to 1.7 million by January 2021, an increase of over 250,000 from the same time the previous year.[2] Free school meals are essential – when delivered properly, they ensure that children receive at least one hot meal a day, irrespective of their situation at home. Sadly, many who would benefit from this guarantee of one hot meal don't receive it, with up to a million UK families in poverty ineligible.[3]

Back when school closures first began, schools and local authorities had to scramble to replace free school meals with a patchwork of provision including food parcels, vouchers and, in some rare instances, cash-based support. Concerns soon began to emerge that some provision was poor quality, overpriced and lacking in nutrition. The messaging over what would be available, and when, was often unclear. Ted could not find out what (if any) support he would receive, and his school seemed equally uncertain:

> Conflicting messages from school this week. Tuesday, 'Dear parent, if you would like a food parcel every two weeks while your child is home learning please let the school know today either by phone or email.'

So I rang them, 'yes please', heard nothing. Thursday, 'We will be issuing free school meals vouchers from next week instead of food parcels. If … you think you may qualify please apply online.' So I emailed to inform them no food parcel this week been given, snotty phone call later that day saying packed lunches are available to collect, where was that mentioned in previous msgs? Friday, 'Dear Parent, we are now issuing vouchers instead of food parcels … They are £12 per week per child so you will receive the first next week.' So now the vouchers are £12 a week ahhhh whatever.

Nellie hit complications, too. Firstly, in confusions about the form that support would take – whether food or cash substitutes. Secondly, about how appropriate any school meal replacements would be:

This is making me so upset. I got in touch with school last week and they were still waiting on the council for information. The school sent out a mass message today saying that anyone who feels they need help with food over the holidays should email them for a food parcel … I'm very worried though. Every family is so different, how can they know what will be useful to us? I have a very picky 5 yr old and a 2 yr old with a milk allergy … They said it would be heavy as it will have a lot of tins. So I dread to think what will be in there. I don't know why they can't just do the £15 a week voucher that other councils/ schools are doing.

As she reflected, the layers of complication and exclusion sent a clear message – that her family's needs weren't important, that life on benefits was not meant to be adequate or easy.

There were also layers of complication around actually converting voucher-based support into food. Barb received vouchers that no retailers could recognise or apply:

My son wasn't in school for several months, and that meant more Xbox use, laptop use and we couldn't use the vouchers that replaced free school meals as they weren't recognised online, by supermarkets.

Facing these difficulties, some parents felt they had little choice but to give up. Ted could barely afford to pay his rent and keep his utilities going; the absence of food support from school led him to risking further debt and potential eviction because he just had nothing else to spare:

I've given up waiting for anything from the school just spent my last £20 on food.

This left Ted unable to put anything in his gas and electricity meters for the ten days until his next Universal Credit payment arrived.

Even when free school meals replacements did come, they were often inadequate. This was highlighted by various parents on Twitter, with one mum pointing out that the food she received to feed her child for ten days would cost just over £5 from local supermarkets, yet private catering company Chartwells were being paid a staggering £30 for the same goods. A tweet by Louisa Britain (aka @roadsidemum) went viral. Alongside a photo of the meagre contents of her free school meals replacement bag, Louisa wrote: 'Issued instead of £30 vouchers. I could do more with £30 to be honest.' Louisa's tweet led to widespread outrage and disgust about the standard of food being offered and about what appeared to be gross profiteering from families on a low income by private companies.

This resonated with Covid Realities parents. Callie, a mum of three, sent us photos of the food she received, along with a description of just how inadequate it was for feeding her children:

I went to collect the food 'hamper' that is supposed to replace 5 days of hot cooked free school meals. Last week the food hampers were labelled woefully inadequate and promises were made to include more food. Well I have even less food than last week. I'm submitting 2 photos, the 1st is the complete food packed for 1 child for 1 week, allegedly worth £15. One of my children is medically diagnosed as lactose intolerant, so the second photo shows what my lactose intolerant son can eat for 5 days of hot school lunch replacement. Basically a 1 egg sandwich, with no margarine or mayo. Half a piece of fruit a day. He can have 3 lots of beans on toast, again no marg. This is disgusting. Please someone highlight how bad this is. Children are going hungry again this week, and still no action is being taken to help them. They are going hungry, and expected to do home schooling work on empty bellies.

But some schools did get it right. When Jenny's school recognised her family's need and sent her a genuinely useful, genuinely bountiful food parcel, she was overjoyed:

> Really overwhelmed that a food parcel arrived today from the children's school. Lots of little treats as well as essentials. Although I'm grateful I'm embarrassed that I'm relying on this and other people must know about it too.

The impossibility of doing schoolwork, at home, on an empty belly re-emphasises just how important such basic provision is. Taya, a parent–teacher–diarist, wrote relatively little about her work. But one thing she did write highlighted the central importance of food to the children she was teaching. She describes the difficulties she faced; the need she saw to provide food aid at a difficult time, and also the additional burdens this placed on teachers, some of whom were also on a low income and struggling to manage rising bills and single parenting:

> I was approached by a parent at my school today who wants to raise funds and food donations for free school meals families over the Christmas break.

I will discuss this with my head teacher over the next few days. Over lockdown we delivered food parcels, presents for the children and vouchers as well as learning packs. I have no idea how we will get these to families if the head agrees, as they will need to be delivered by staff due to GDPR [General Data Protection Regulations] etc but over Christmas I think we will all just need a break and I can't do it alone. But some of our families rely on such gestures. Our school harvest festival was cancelled, it should have been this week. I had a last minute bid to save it when I found out, but the Salvation Army had already been cancelled and the head said we did not have covid safe capacity for it. I can't help but think of how many recipients won't be receiving these this year.

Taya's diary entry highlights the stresses and strains, the community spirit and the difficult decisions of lockdown – but through all of it runs a central element: food. Food was a persistent, unavoidable cost for overstretched families and it impacted on relationships with schools.

Even with all the problems with free school meal replacements, they were still better than nothing. But nothing was what it looked like families would get during the school holidays, until intervention came from an unlikely place – Manchester United striker Marcus Rashford. In June 2020, Premier League footballer Marcus Rashford emerged as a high-profile campaigner for the provision of free school meals replacements during holidays. He argued that, without this, families who were already facing new financial pressures could go hungry.

Despite the efforts of charities, campaigners and academics, it took a Manchester United footballer to convince the government to provide vouchers in the summer holidays for children in England who were receiving free school meals in term time. And he had to campaign again, come the autumn, as the government yet again resisted demands to continue free school meals replacements outside of term time. Rashford's determination paid off, with him pushing the government into a U-turn that saw them provide free school meals replacements in the Christmas 2020 and Easter and Summer 2021 school holidays.

These U-turns were rightly celebrated, but they still left gaps and holes in provision, and there is a strong case to be made that Marcus Rashford should be much more ambitious in his campaign efforts. His stated aim is to end child food poverty, but this is only a small part of what needs to be done. It's about putting in measures to address poverty – full stop. Rashford's campaign drew attention to the extent and impact of poverty, an issue that has consistently remained low on the government's agenda. This is a good thing. But his narrow focus on food should raise concerns about the ongoing fragmentation of poverty that we see in the UK, where the problem of poverty is divided into various poverty types: period poverty, hygiene poverty, furniture poverty, pet poverty, funeral poverty ... The list is apparently endless. There is a danger that a narrow focus on (child) food poverty suggests that a solution can be found in providing people with more food, obscuring the underpinning issue of a lack of financial security. We can see why this matters as we move on to look in more detail at experiences of schooling in the pandemic, experiences that were profoundly shaped by the extent of the poverty that families faced.

An end to home schooling?

Home schooling in lockdown was not easy for anyone. The suddenness of being expected to teach your child, all day every day, often while juggling the care of other children and your own paid employment, regularly felt impossible. I don't think any of us wanted to become teachers overnight, taking on responsibility for getting children logged onto their Zooms, helping them with their tricky maths problems and the demands of a new curriculum that many of us find impossible to understand. But, in the face of a national crisis, we had no choice.

For parents taking part in Covid Realities, though, navigating home schooling was often made more difficult because of their poverty, something which was not sufficiently addressed by the government or – in many cases – by over-stretched schools. The charity Action for Children[4] flagged the significance of the 'digital divide' for families hit hardest by the pandemic, who often struggled to access devices or get online and participate in home education. Erik was one such parent:

> Life is a real struggle to survive at the moment. I finally have internet connection again today after 2 weeks without connection and my daughter unable to do her online learning. People on low incomes really need more financial help from the government.

The cost of broadband was enough to leave Erik struggling to meet his monthly bills and keep himself and his daughter warm and properly clothed.

Everyday financial hardship was made worse by the additional costs that came with home learning. For families living on a low income, these extra demands placed real pressures on already stretched budgets. Nellie's child's school seemed unaware of how these pressures played out at home:

> School sent work for my daughter to do, but we couldn't access it as my husband uses the computer for his work. Pretty pointless really … School sent round a questionnaire, and we told them we only had one laptop, which is used for work, but they don't seem to have acted on it. I'm personally not too bothered as it's only reception and she's bright and ahead anyway, but I did get a nagging email from her teacher stressing how important it was she did the work set, even after I explained about the computer situation. It's also assumed we have a printer (we do but it doesn't always have ink or paper).

Many parents simply had no spare resources for home schooling, and sometimes felt that schools did not take much (or any) account of this. While schools could not directly provide broadband, some failed to recognise that an absence of broadband meant additional support of other kinds was needed – for example, providing hard copies of schoolwork rather than requiring it all to be completed online. As Andrea wrote:

> I am in the lowest 10% of the income and I struggled immensely with having no wifi ... I felt I was 'inconveniencing' the school by requesting more paper resource.

As many of us recall, home schooling also created additional demands on our time: time which for families in poverty was often in short supply. Ted felt pressure from his daughter's school during home schooling, pressure which cut across and sat alongside the pressure to keep his house and daughter warm:

> During the first lockdown I had some woman from supposedly school attendance coming to [my] door in her car. [My daughter] had to wave out of the window (I had a feeling of being singled out). Even though I took her work out she did not want to see it ... School have a timetable, every task completed [there has] got to be [a] photo sent ASAP throughout the day or scanned in so they can check the online learning side of things. [T]hat's added pressure on parents and time consuming. When ya sitting worrying about keeping this house warm ... I really am in a panic.

During periods of home schooling, some children still attended school in person: the children of key workers and those classed as 'vulnerable'. Government guidance set out that vulnerable children for these purposes included:

> those who may have difficulty engaging with remote education at home (for example due to a lack of devices or quiet space to study).

But while this expansive understanding of vulnerability was written into the guidance, it did not regularly translate into provision, at least for the parents taking part in Covid Realities. Instead, they were routinely left to struggle on with home schooling, juggling additional financial and time pressures as a result. Notably, survey research by Child Poverty Action Group

tomorrow's
future
family
change
WORRIED
HELP!
Don't forget us!
tomorrow
We
NEED
Opportunity

found that 40% of families on a low income said they were missing at least one essential resource required for home schooling. This will have left a long legacy, both in the stresses it placed on families during lockdown, and on the inequitable impact on missed educational opportunities.

In this way, home schooling created new divisions between richer and poorer families. When schools reopened their gates it was to children whose home schooling experiences were shaped by these educational inequalities. The return of schools gave some families hope; but for others it was a time of anxiety and fear.

'I do have a feeling of dread every day ...' Back at the school gates

The start of a new school year in August and September 2020, and with it an end to home schooling, brought with it mixed feelings. Some parents agonised over whether or not to send their children in at all, pondering, as did Teddie, whether home schooling might be kinder:

> The turmoil in my head of 'do I send my children to school?' (3 have [Education Health and Care Plans] and one a support plan). Only getting two hours' sleep after having a battle with myself on what to do for the best educationally, socially wise for the children.

But there were parents who also felt joy – relief at the prospect of reclaimed time, of a chance to be an independent adult again. Aubrey told us:

> It was like heaven dropping the kids to school the first day. It gave me a chance to go shopping and clean the house.

Tahlia's world was reopening, too. Her children would be able to see their friends; she would be able to see other adults again for the first time in months:

I'm so grateful schools opened again. My children missed their friends terribly, it badly affected their wellbeing. Their faces changed into happiness the day they returned … We no longer live in a ground hog day of isolation … I missed people so much.

Feelings about the return to school were often mixed, even within the same family. Syeda's eldest daughter longed for the return of her social life, and the chance to be 'normal' again:

Her first year as a teenager has been surreal and she misses her friends. She is usually very sociable … Even she saw it as a blessing to get back to school.

However, the self-same return came at a cost for his youngest whose struggles with the return were exacerbated by the loss of dedicated support services:

She loved being off school and so going back really affected her … Even before this year she had not been invited to a birthday party for 5yrs. The school cannot devote resources or a safe space to the club for pupils with social difficulties she used to attend. So her attendance is down, and she is struggling to engage.

Parents with children in this kind of position described real tensions – recognising that their child might feel more comfortable at home, but that this could lead them to long-term problems with social development.

It felt important that this came at the end of a long period of uncertainty, too. All children, but particularly those with additional needs, benefit from structure, and COVID uprooted many familiar routines. Schedules were discarded as lockdowns kicked in and school disappeared, and providing predictability – in houses struggling even to provide certainty around heating or food – proved relentlessly hard. Charlotte, a trained teacher, was concerned that local schools had not:

put any measures in place to deal with the stress and anxiety and uncertainty the children have had because of lockdown. It appears the schools went back as if nothing happened and the emotions children exhibited were swept under the carpet.

This emotional side felt essential: it was not just the processes of learning and of social interaction that COVID took away, but the structure to days and, indeed, to the progression of young lives. Tough times became tougher as school restarted. And all of this instability and anxiety was within the context of the costs and burdens of a new school year.

'Nothing really makes sense no more!' Schools return, as colleges and universities stay online

As schools reopened their gates many parents, including myself, worried about sending their children into an environment in which COVID would surely spread, and quickly. Helen wrote in her diary that she found

> school ... a worrying time. Children mixing in large groups, going to outside activities again. We are seeing birthday parties start up again, and the rise in cases.

Inconsistencies in the system also worried parents. It was hard to understand why the risks of transmission were being managed in universities and workplaces, while schools appeared to be treated as a separate, inexplicably low-risk, entity. Teddie explained:

> I cannot get my head round how college can run at 50% capacity, have most work online, and through zoom type meetings ... yet my younger children can attend school, be in year group bubbles and be more exposed than they have been in six months ... Nothing really makes sense no more!

To parents like Teddie, the sense of confused and contradictory policy stood out – decisions that appeared to make no sense, based on evidence that was unclear.

For some parents, the risks of school also held added significance. Tilly told us that if her daughter brought COVID home she would have to stop work:

> I worry as [my daughter] has to travel to & from school – who she is mixing with etc in case she gets Covid & brings it back home for me to have to close my business & no income 😷😊

Tilly could see the risks confronting her family, with the return of schooling a new pathway for picking up infection. In Tilly's account we see how the fear of contracting COVID-19 intersected with fears of losing income as a result, layering worry on top of worry, stress on top of stress.

For parents of pre-school children, access to childcare, and to some respite from the endless caring work of parenthood, depended a lot on where in the UK you lived. Nurseries and early years settings remained open for much of the pandemic in England, for example, while Scotland took a much more cautious approach. Nellie, who lives in England, was grateful that her nursery reopened in the summer of 2020. She explained:

> We have been so lucky with my daughter's nursery provider. Not only do we absolutely love them anyway because they totally value and reflect our style of parenting and attitude to the outdoors (it's a Forest School). But when they closed due to Covid and chose not to open during June when they were technically allowed to, they instead chose to open at the end of July and throughout August (they're usually term time only). Because [my daughter's] place is funded and they continued to receive that funding during the closure, she has been able to go over the summer at no cost to us. It's been wonderful for her. Some independent time for her, away from

her baby brother, and in preparation for starting school. And it's given me a bit of a break too. We're going to really miss it come September.

Other parents were not so fortunate. Daniela set out the impact on her and her children:

> The new lockdown which started in January came as a shock. Children were not ready for the news and it took time to make them understand why they can't go to school and nursery. It is very stressful time as having to help kids with remote learning seems very hectic. It become[s] even harder when kids are very young. Coping with mental health is another level of struggle … Overall it is very distressful time.

It was not always easy to understand the differences in restrictions, and this added to the worries that parents faced as they tried to support their children with transitions between being at home full-time and the reopening of nurseries and schools.

'School uniform … We had to apply for our second crisis loan'

Anxieties about school were amplified by the additional costs that came with it. Whenever schools returned after a lockdown we saw wave after wave of parents writing about how anxious they were at the costs of the new school term – and of school uniform, in particular. Despite extensive planning and budgeting, the costs of many uniforms are completely unmanageable for those on limited budgets.[5] Just one uniform took over half of Alannah's total monthly income:

> Am anxious and financially broke, paying £310 for school uniform. When I only receive £556 a month.

Many Covid Realities parents described having to choose between heating or eating because of the financial pressure put on them by buying uniforms. Andrea explained:

> With ever increasing cost regarding food, electricity
> and gas I am struggling now with a brand-new
> uniform for my eldest child ... It's just money, money,
> money in already stressful and difficult times.

Parents prioritised school uniforms within their household
budgets. Uniforms took precedence over birthday presents for
Dotty's family, and drove her to seek out a crisis loan:

> We have had birthdays this week. Unfortunately,
> we couldn't afford presents etc. We received emails
> through from our daughter's school ... [W]e can't
> afford to buy her school uniform. We had to apply
> for our 2nd crisis loan.

With a fair few parents describing tense relationships with their
schools, fears of their children being excluded or punished
left parents prioritising uniform alongside, or even above,
other essentials.

Making this harder still, many families' usual strategies for
buying uniforms had become impossible. Tahlia once relied on
charity shops and hand-me-downs from friends and family for
uniforms. She couldn't access these during lockdown, triggering
a spiral of bills, debt and hunger:

> Before covid I would see my brother every few
> months, and he would give us hand-me-down
> clothes ... A few mums would do the same. Because
> of covid ... I've not received any hand-me-down
> clothes for my sons this whole year ... In September
> had to buy 3 children all brand new uniform ...
> I'm £2000 in debt, I ran out of money a week last
> Thursday ... I ran out of food over last weekend ...
> I've only eaten a diet based on bread and potatoes
> this last month as I wanted to ensure my kids had
> food. I was becoming nutrient deficient.

That school uniform is competing with food in families'
budgeting reflects the extent of hardship that so many families

face, and also the unreasonable (and for too many unmanageable) expense of kitting your child out for school. These are costs for which families do not receive support. Indeed, up to 80% of English local authorities offer low-income families no support[6] with the costs of uniform. Scotland[7] and Wales[8] guarantee more generous uniform grants, and Northern Ireland provides some financial support.[9]

Still, Ayda applied to her Scottish local authority well in advance, but heard nothing by the time the costs of uniform arrived:

> I applied to our local authority for a school clothing grant & free school meals 4 weeks ago & I still have not received any word on the outcome ... Feeling very let down by our local authority.

Teddie found she was ineligible because of the benefits she received:

> I saw advertised about uniform grants and thought 'oh great we must be able to apply' WRONG!!!! 'No,' yet again because of the working tax credit ...

And for those who did receive them, uniform grants were consistently inadequate for the costs they were meant to cover. Many did not even cover the cost of a blazer, as Andrea shared:

> The uniform is a few hundred pounds. The uniform grant is £73 or thereabouts. That doesn't even cover the price of a blazer.

Uniform, then, was a debilitating cost at an expensive time, which left parents balancing the stresses of the return to school with the anxiety stemming from the financial pressures it created. Advocates of school uniform often describe how it should encourage 'uniformity' in schools, with those with fewer financial resources not subject to the stigma that can come with not being able to afford to wear the right (and often expensive) brands of trainers and clothes. And this is right! But, too often, badged and needlessly expensive uniforms are eating up large chunks of the budgets of families experiencing poverty. More needs to be done to make school uniforms affordable. New legislation in England[10] stipulating that local authorities must now develop statutory guidance on school uniform costs is a welcome development. But we also need to look more broadly at why families are left in a situation where they simply cannot find room in their budget for these essential purchases. This problem is much deeper than the price of school uniforms, and has to do with fundamental problems with our social security system.

The costs of going to school

The return of schools also brought a return to the additional costs of schooling, which all too often extend beyond school uniform to fundraising, school trips and pressures to have the 'right' stationery or risk feeling left out and excluded. The additional costs of the school day create inevitable financial pressures for families. There is a pressing need for schools to have greater awareness of the impact that requests for additional money from parents and carers can have, and the extent to which even small amounts can place a very big burden on those experiencing poverty.

At worst, schools could assume access to money in ways that left children openly shamed. Nellie's five-year-old was reduced to tears by having her poverty emphasised in front of her whole class:

> Recently they were raising funds and gave us the opportunity to purchase a mug with our child's drawing on it. I didn't order one, we don't have the money to spare. Yesterday my 5 yr old came home crying because every single other child in her class was given a mug at home time and she didn't have one. Why oh why couldn't they give them out discreetly!

The depth of Nellie's anger reflected the pain of her situation – seeing her own daughter humiliated for reasons well beyond her family's control. It also reflects a failure of the school to be sensitive to the diversity of family circumstances within their school community; more needs to be done here to support the whole school community.

Prior to the pandemic, there had been a growing emphasis on efforts to 'poverty proof the school day', an approach pioneered and then rolled out by Children North East.[11] The charity, based in the North of England, found that schools were often unintentionally stigmatising those who lived in families on a low income. The charity explained that:

> too often in schools, children living in poverty are unintentionally stigmatised, discriminated against, left out or excluded ... It extends to school trips where some children are excluded because of the cost, or unable to pick something up from the gift shop on the way out even when they can afford to go ... We have also learned that pupils can be given a detention for not being able to afford stationery or ingredients for food technology lessons, which then makes them miss the school bus when there is no alternative way of getting home.

Children North East now works in partnership with Child Poverty Action Group to support schools to audit their practices to 'poverty proof' the school day, using available resources, like pupil premium money, to reduce the potential stigma that children can face because of their family's poverty. The impact of COVID-19 has made this work even more important.

'Atishoo, atishoo, we all fall down!' Schools as sites of infection

It is hard to find data on how many school bubbles burst. During the pandemic, the Office for National Statistics reported on the proportion of children testing positive for COVID-19 in any three-week period – one in every 150 primary school children and one in every 2,000 secondary school children in the three weeks to 21 May 2021. They also reported on the proportion of children with antibodies (suggesting exposure to COVID either through vaccination or infection), and this varied considerably across the country – from one in 20 children in Bournemouth and Norfolk to one in four in Manchester and in Barking and Dagenham. However, this is not a reflection of the levels of disruption caused – some children may be asymptomatic, while one symptomatic child could result in a bubble of five, ten, 15 children being sent home for a mandatory ten days of self-isolation. My six-year-old neighbour had her school bubble burst four times; my son's burst just once. The entire secondary school just up the road closed early for the 2021 summer break because nearly every year group had been decimated by burst bubbles and positive tests.

When dried corn reaches about 180 degrees Celsius, it begins to pop. First one isolated kernel, then another; and soon the whole pan is popping merrily away. This pattern mirrored the experiences of parents watching their children's schools – first one positive test, then another, with the positive tests getting closer and closer. As local COVID levels rose, Christopher saw this beginning to happen in his daughter's school, nudging his anxiety higher:

> The area I live is moving up to tier 2 tonight due to rising cases in the area, there has also been another confirmed case at my daughter's school today which I am finding a bit concerning.

Helen's first pop, meanwhile, came from a school cleaner:

> With schools back on Monday and cases rising in our local small town it's looking likely school is going to see classroom cases. They have only had 1 and it was a cleaner so no children sent home yet …

Then, slowly at first, school bubbles began to burst. Very few of the parents taking part in Covid Realities had children test positive in the first year of the pandemic, but many of them experienced the challenges of bursting bubbles. Teachers, cleaners, children and dinner ladies were all identified as the source of children's popped bubbles, often with significant consequences at home. For Ted, it was his daughter's dinner lady; and the extra costs of home schooling he could no longer bear:

> A dinner lady tests positive so we [are] self-isolating, back to home schooling. I know it's only 14 days but on my mind is the extra gas, electric, fridge raids i.e. snacks … 10 days left to go.

Aurora's son's bubble burst when another child fell ill. Again, it wasn't just the threat of illness or burdens of home schooling – burst bubbles also meant yet more unaffordable costs:

> We're expected to shop and book delivery slots, of which all are already booked far in advance. Another issue is the cost for delivery in itself. This can be the difference between having a couple of meals or not. Back into isolation we go.

Worries over the extra cost that self-isolation would bring caused additional distress to families on a low income, such as Nellie's:

> I'm dreading my daughter's school bubble bursting. We just can't afford it. Not only the loss of work, but also the increased cost of lunch and constant snacking. We've had to isolate as a family twice now, because of my 2-year-old developing a temperature and having a test. Both times were negative but we had to wait 5 days each time for the results. That's what makes me infuriated. The results need to come faster. Five days is too long to wait, and has a big negative effect financially.

In Nellie's account, we see the fear of self-isolation and of getting ill (which most of us faced) collide with worries about how they would cope with the resultant financial fallout.

What the diary entries of both Aurora and Nellie remind us of is that while many of us can relate to the rollercoaster of bubbles bursting and scrabbling to cope with subsequent isolation and an often unwelcome return to home schooling, some households also experienced greater financial precarity and fear around how to navigate additional expenses. Each time a bubble burst, families experiencing poverty had both new routines and new expenses to manage, creating additional strain for already stretched households. This everyday reality was once again totally neglected in the policy response. Families facing burst bubbles were left unsupported as they sought to find room in their tight budgets for the additional costs of a spell of self-isolation: costs of feeding children lunch, of increased energy use, and of trying to keep them occupied.

The financial screws also tightened when burst bubbles interrupted the ability of parents to go to work. A single parent, Thea needed her self-employed income to stay afloat. Repeated burst bubbles – without any government support – pushed her to the edge of financial survival:

> Since September my son has had to isolate twice due to coming into contact with someone with covid in his school bubble. With this, because I'm not having to personally isolate, it seems I can't claim anything to help when I'm having to stay off work to take care of my son.

Burdens of care compounded the position of families like Thea's. Caring commitments meant parents had less flexibility to play with when bubbles burst.

And through all of these difficulties, children with additional needs were hit especially hard. Charlie felt that all the tensions of single parenting in lockdown were compressed when his daughter's bubble burst:

> We are now self-isolating after a positive result for my middle daughter ... Am finding it hard to cope locked up again with my daughters at home, one of which has special needs ... The hardest thing I find is home schooling, keeping the house tidy and myself

sane, life's hard enough as a single father but in lock downs it's made even harder.

For Charlie, staying on top of supporting his children meant that some other necessities of life (cleaning, tidying and managing his own well-being) soon became impossible.

Teddie, too, found that burst bubbles complicated support for the multiple and competing needs of her children. Again, additional needs made it harder to communicate sudden changes:

> My 7 year old ... has been on the waiting list for over a year for an ADHD assessment. This two week isolation has turned his little world upside down, he can't concentrate, the change in routine is killing him and trying to get him to do his work is like trying to get blood from a stone – impossible. Trying to make him understand why he isn't allowed out when his siblings can is another story!

'It's a parent's worst nightmare and I worry for the future for our children'

The Guardian describes today's school children as a generation 'at risk',[12] setting out an expectation that lost schooling could cost their generation £350 billion in lifetime earnings.[13] As ever, this impact will be skewed – it is the poorest who risk losing the most. This taps into ideas of a 'lost generation' of children – of those who have missed so much school that they may never be able to get back on track. This was a key concern for Covid Realities parents; as Howie commented, 'I am concerned about education inequality growing.' Parents experiencing poverty felt left behind as they saw other families stream ahead of them, making use of resources that they could never hope to access. Private tuition, for instance, was beyond Nicole's budget:

> As school is unable to supply a tutor for maths for my daughter, I enquired at the Kip McGrath centre. £32 for 80 mins maths tuition ... I cannot afford this.

Even though she was a qualified teacher, Charlotte felt there was no way she could help her children to catch up on all that they had missed:

> My biggest fear is the future of our children. Their education has suffered and I'm still trying to help my 2 children catch up on all those lost months of work.

For some unlucky children, lockdown happened in a critical exam year. Across multiple parents' accounts, there was a real sense of the unfairness about the uncertainty this triggered – hitting vulnerable children hardest:

> This new lockdown has brought uncertainty and anxiety for 2 of my children who were due to take BTEC exams in the next couple of weeks ... It's still unclear how their coursework assessments will be affected given that they'll miss half a term of college and the practicals they need to do for their science diplomas.

The basics of Covid schooling, then, gave the lie to the claim that 'we are all in this together'. Families in poverty faced persistent barriers as they tried to support their children with schooling through the pandemic, barriers that could have been dismantled through targeted government intervention. We have seen how this intervention was so often missing and how when it did come – most notably in free school meal replacements during the school holidays – it was only because of the campaigning efforts of Marcus Rashford. The legacy of the failure of the government to properly support families in poverty during the pandemic will be a long one, and it will likely include a widening of the gap in socioeconomic educational inequalities.

Reframing 'anti-poverty action' as 'pro-education policy'

Schooling is presented as a free good – a public service, with the education of young people benefiting us all. As the UK has moved to a post-industrial service economy, the drive for children to stay in school for longer, and for a greater percentage to go to university, has boomed. However, the continued dominance of privately educated people in almost every sphere of public life is well documented. Privately educated people (just 7% of the UK's population[14]) make up 65% of judges, 57% of Members of the House of Lords and 52% of the Westminster Government's diplomats and junior ministers. Parental privilege and social class plays a huge role within the state sector too – it is no accident that the state school that consistently produces the highest levels of Oxbridge admittance is Hills Road, a sixth form college in Cambridge. Access to private tutoring creates further divisions within state-educated cohorts, and children in receipt of free school meals are seriously disadvantaged in their fight for good grades and decent post-school opportunities.

Through Covid Realities, we saw how the pandemic further exposed and extended these inequalities; how disruption to school prevented children from accessing basic resources, interrupted their relationships with schools and set them back still further compared to their more privileged peers. During the pandemic, we have also seen how privilege significantly impacted on the schooling you might receive, even during lockdowns. For example, one survey found that 74% of privately educated children benefited from full, virtual school days during the first lockdown of Spring 2020, compared with just 38% of state school pupils.[15] School disruption also drove intersecting insecurities, making the everyday lives of families in poverty only harder still. A burst bubble immediately meant extra costs – of heating, electricity, food and materials. For some parents, a burst bubble also resulted in loss of work, hitting low-wage earners hard at the time when they could least afford it. However, school also brought with it additional costs that felt much harder to bear because of the stop–start nature of lockdown. Uniforms represented an especially big financial hit, and purchasing them often left families struggling and sometimes unable to meet their basic financial needs.

Across all of this cuts the deep financial insecurity faced by the parents taking part in Covid Realities. No matter which way they turned, they simply lacked the financial resources they and their families needed. The message from this is clear: if we value education, families in poverty must be lifted out of it so that their children can be supported to thrive in schools. To place a meaningful value on free education, meaningful social security must underpin it.

Chapter four
Christmas in the pandemic

Led by Geoff

Christmas 2020 was a far cry from the joyous occasion I had pictured. Myself and my husband were tired, emotionally and physically, from spending the year protecting our vulnerable children. Both my children were born with chronic lung disease, and although growing healthier by the day, the pandemic gripped us in a fear like no other. Like many others, we did not know the full impact of what may happen if Covid-19 took hold of them, or indeed, us. We followed guidelines and relied upon shielding to protect us. We survived on food parcels, grocery drop-offs, vouchers and anything we could lay our hands on just to get by. Fearful for the future, we dared not think about tomorrow, and instead focused on the day ahead. So there was real hope when the Prime Minister declared on National Television that Britain WOULD in fact be able to see loved ones from outside of their home on Christmas Day. However, this joy was short-lived. The government declared a U-turn on its promise.

Fiona

Christmas 2020 and the only thing piling up under our tree was sadness, worry, guilt, heartbreak and shame. We couldn't afford the 'perfect' Christmas, the one shoved down our throats from the adverts. We could barely afford heating and everyday food. Our Christmas was a few gifts for my children that were all second hand and a make-do dinner made up of forgotten bits of food scraped from the back of the freezer. There was no extended family over to visit due to the covid lockdown. We used hot water bottles and blankets to keep warm as we couldn't afford to have the heating on for too long and we spent most of the day watching films on TV. There was none of the normal laughter, madness or messiness that comes with a full house on Christmas day. We did our best to keep our spirits up and keep the magic alive but when the house is cold, there isn't a lavish meal to sit down to, no extended family allowed to visit you, your children are confused as to why Santa didn't bring them what was on their lists, and you are wracked with guilt and shame, it is extremely difficult.

Lexie

'Thank goodness the Christmas day farce is over.' Alex's Christmas

For Alex, a single parent from Scotland, the first signs of Christmas 2020 began early. In the midst of a health scare, Christmas loomed as the next big threat to her well-being:

> The next big C word is Christmas. It's in our faces in shops, on TV and on social media. Perfect families in perfect homes, crackling open fire and smiling faces. I will be on my own with my child, who has expectations that I cannot afford. It's added pressure I don't need.

The messages were incessant, and everywhere: that Christmas was coming, that Christmas was a time of joy, and that Christmas was a time of excess. Alex couldn't avoid them, and the message they sent reminded her of the challenges of her situation:

> The Council has put up the street Xmas lights. Adverts on tv, radio and social media for gifts to buy. Anxiety is rising from the pit of my stomach. Each year I am reminded that as a single parent on low income, how worthless I am.

Still, Alex tried her best, looking for opportunities to make the most of Christmas. Seeing a present in a charity shop, she went for it only for a chance encounter to emphasise the poverty and the shame that accompanied it.

> Saw a wicker basket in charity shop, bought it to fill with toiletries for my daughter as a Xmas gift. As I came out the shop, I bumped into [an acquaintance]. She looked at me, at the shop and back to me, with disgust written all over her face ... Oh to have the support of grandparents to do childcare for free, to go and work as a teacher ... I'm 24hrs a day 7 days a week. No childcare from grandparents, no wealthy husband ... Some people have no idea ...

Here, we see how the stigma of poverty plays out in social settings. Who knows if Alex's acquaintance was disgusted by her presence in a charity shop? Or if, instead, it is Alex's own feelings of shame at her poverty that led her to assume the disgust of her acquaintance.

Without any financial headroom, justifying spending on Christmas felt difficult for Alex. Any additional money had to go straight on the necessities of life:

> Received £100 from Scottish Gov for Xmas. Tempted to buy something extra for my daughter. Did an online food shop instead. No fancy cheese, wine or pate ... Washing powder, toilet roll, diluting juice ... lots of it, and more tins than a foodbank.

The day itself offered no respite.

> Thank goodness the Christmas day farce is over. My daughter spent it in her room avoiding me. Nobody phoned or messaged to wish us a Merry Christmas or if we were ok.

As the New Year approached, Alex's experience of Christmas left her feeling worse than ever. What is typically framed as a time of joy and of celebrations was, for Alex, a reminder of her poverty and isolation.

In the early 19th century, Victorian reformers introduced the concept of 'less eligibility'. The idea, written into law in 1834, was to ensure that the quality of life in the workhouse was worse than the meanest quality of life outside. The intention was to deter people from accessing support. The same principle lives on today in the idea that 'work should always pay' – that dependence on social security for all or part of one's income should always be 'less eligible' than life in paid employment. The 'less eligibility' principle is underpinned by the idea that, without it, people would too easily and quickly choose benefits (or the workhouse, historically) over paid work.

The passivity and inactivity that is so often assumed to characterise people on benefits contrasts with the very real, and very hard, work that getting by on benefits involves. This chapter unpacks how all this plays out in the context of family celebrations, especially Christmas. It sets out how families in poverty consistently find themselves excluded from aspects of very public consumption and struggle to manage children's expectations that life (and Father Christmas) is in some (or any) way equitable, or just. This chapter, like every chapter in this book, also makes clear just how much work is undertaken by parents in poverty, budgeting carefully and creatively finding ways to make celebratory moments special when money is tight.

The ghost of Christmases past

Alex's experiences were sadly far from unique. Many Covid Realities families faced the challenge of navigating what in many ways is a celebration of consumption when they were finding it hard enough just getting by. No one gets targeted ads for their birthday, no one expects much come Father's Day. But shopping and consumption are central to modern Christmas festivities.[1]

As early as the mid-1800s, Dickens saw in the abundance of Christmas – the feasting, the celebrations, the extravagance – a useful backdrop for social critique. In *A Christmas Carol* the selfish, penny-pinching Ebenezer Scrooge symbolises all that is wrong with money-worshipping greed. In contrast to Scrooge, there is his impoverished employee, Bob Cratchit, and his seriously disabled son, Tiny Tim, who may die unless Scrooge changes his ways.

A hundred and eighty years on, the contrasts and inequalities laid out by Dickens persist. We have already seen in Chapters 1 and 2 the experiences of families struggling, often daily, to get by as they faced 'less eligibility' in action. Christmas inevitably magnifies this, and can make it harder to bear. As Meg reflected,

> Xmas [is] going to be a bit of a muted affair this year, not that it has ever been extravagant in previous years due to lack of money.

Other parents described the problems that Christmas could cause. In August, Syeda was still 'in debt for the console and clothes and Christmas/birthdays from last year', while Ted had always felt pressured to live up to his daughter's view of him as a 'superman' – perfect, strong, endlessly coping.

This will be familiar to many of us: the pressure to live up to expectations, often unrealistic, and to make things as perfect as they can be. Many families in Covid Realities relied on the summer months to see them through between the significant annual expenses of winter heating costs, culminating in Christmas. With the tough conditions of 2020, few had been able to recover from Christmas 2019 before the next round of winter expenses arrived.

First thoughts about Christmas

How do you celebrate at a social distance? This was a problem many of us confronted during the pandemic. In the run-up to Christmas 2020 this problem was complicated by uncertainty about what we would be allowed to do: there was also the question about what we were willing to do. At certain points it looked as though we would be allowed to visit other people in 'Christmas bubbles', but rising levels of infection and hospitalisation made the wisdom of this look questionable. For families on low incomes, these problems were added to the perennial problem of a Christmas without enough money. As Charlotte put it:

> It's that time of year again when I worry sick about providing a decent Christmas for my children on Universal Credit. While toys are not an essential thing, children do not know that.

Parents faced the difficult task of trying to find extra when even the basics weren't covered. Christmas wasn't a single, lonely bump in an otherwise clear financial road, but came as the end point of a long and difficult year. In June and July, parents wrote about the added costs of lockdown and home schooling (see Chapters 1 and 3). In August, they were hit by the costs of school uniforms, described in Chapter 3. By September and October, they were crumbling under the costs of winter. By the time Christmas approached, these additional financial pressures left families facing an increasingly impossible struggle to get by.

This meant that families had to look ahead. Even in early October, Ted was beginning to plan – but his Christmas had to compete with the costs of basic clothing:

> [My daughter] needs a winter coat, tights, etc for school then there is the FAT man coming (Santa Claus). Can't even bear thinking about it.

It wasn't *just* that costs were rising, emotional stresses and strains had built up over the preceding year, too. By early December, it had accumulated into a heap of anxieties for Callie:

> I don't think I have ever felt as anxious about Christmas as I do this year … the whole thing, the lack of family, the lack of my children's dad, the complete lack of money … the whole thing is so much pressure just on me.

And Christmas brought some unique pressures. It was one stress that parents just could not share with their children – particularly when it came to Santa. Lexie explained:

> It's not like my kids are too young to understand the concept of Christmas and the magic, but they are not old enough to understand that the pressure is on the parents, not Santa!!

From September onwards, then, Christmas presented parents with a growing sense of worry and the need to find money they did not have.

It is common for your loved ones to try to protect you when the pressure is on – not wanting to ask for something when time or money is short. We saw this play out at Christmas time, with older children asking only for modest gifts (or none at all) in an effort to protect their parents from their poverty. Alex described her teenage daughter's reluctance to ask for Christmas presents she knew she could not afford:

> Asked my daughter what she would like for
> Christmas. She shook her head ... said she doesn't
> know. ... that means she does but doesn't want to say
> in case it stresses me out, as she knows I can't afford
> what she would like.

Though it was still difficult, for older children 'austerity Christmas' could at least be explained. It was the younger children – with their expectations of a just and equitable Father Christmas – who had the toughest explanations ahead of them. Andrea's children covered the divide, and she told us:

> It's not presents I am worried about as I've already
> informed my 11 year old who knows about Santa ...
> that she may get IOU notes and some money for
> Jan[uary] ... It's the wee 7-year-old boy. He doesn't
> know why Covid is restricting Santa's access.

For these parents of young children, the 'magic' that is meant to come with Christmas made it even harder to recalibrate expectations. Being seen as 'less eligible' by Santa was a hard message indeed.

'Spending has been frequent and a lot.' Finding a budget for Christmas

Broadly, sensible money management can be understood as 'financial capability', with key behaviours being

> budgeting, precautionary saving, prudent borrowing,
> seeking free debt advice early in the event of
> difficulties, following through a debt solution, and
> using the right information in decisions, for instance,
> about credit scores.[2]

When my wife and I[3] separated, my monthly income disappeared into a black hole of mortgages, emergency rent and living expenses, meaning that each month started with a balance of minus £300. Of course, I watched the price of everything

– each penny coming in and going out, filling the car £5 at a time, looking for deals. On the rare occasions we went out, my son had the chippie's £3.50 fish strips with chips; I had his leftovers. Our finances got worse, and worse, and worse. It wasn't my planning at fault, it was the sheer lack of finances that I had to be capable with. During this period, I did more financial planning than I'd ever done in my life: spending my time and energy trying to work out how to make ends meet.

Parents and carers told us repeatedly of their financial capability, their strategies to save a few pence on food shopping, to put money aside for crises or to survive a difficult month. This reflects a central paradox around ideas of financial capability and another, linked buzzword: financial resilience. There is often a suggestion that those living on low incomes need to get better at budgeting and be supported to improve and extend their financial capabilities. But in fact, as research study after research study shows, people in poverty are highly creative and effective at budgeting small sums of money: doing the best they can to get by without enough.[4]

We see this play out in how parents planned for Christmas. Victoria, for instance, used supermarket credit to smooth out the gap between pay days and ensure she could afford a Christmas meal:

> When I got sent some money last week ... I immediately bought several vouchers from Aldi. That way on 23/24th we can take a trip to buy Christmas Dinner items without worrying if the money will still be in my account.

Linked to the idea of financial capability is another paradox: that those with the least often pay more for the basics, known as the 'poverty premium'.[5] Families in poverty frequently have to pay more for electricity and gas, through expensive pre-payment meters; and more for basic food items from a local shop, rather than from less accessible but cheaper supermarkets.

In the run-up to Christmas 2020, we saw the poverty premium in action. For example, while catalogues could help spread out costs, they did so by offering long-term loans at punitive interest rates. We saw Helen managing Christmas this way; catalogues allowed her to buy her daughter a big present, but the cost had to be paid over nine long months:

> Normally I would have started buying in August, this year I haven't been able to … My child's main present is being bought on a 9 month payment from a catalogue, the rest I have to gather up any spare change to buy them.

Despite this extensive (and early) budgeting for Christmas, Helen was still left feeling anxious about how she'd afford the remaining gifts for her daughter:

> My girl is 9 so still believes in Santa. Don't we all. She hasn't done her list and it's worrying, I don't want to disappoint her … I'm hoping after Christmas things will begin to look better.

Counterbalancing saving strategies were cost-cutting measures. Dorothy exemplified this approach, explaining how she had to trim every imaginable cost to create some capacity for present buying:

> It's definitely getting colder. I'm not even having the heating on a lot … I still have presents to buy … So I'm just really literally not buying as much food or as much luxuries a week but you still need to buy the essentials so usually you can only stretch it so far.

This experience was not universal, though. Che's loss of work meant her family could barely survive – and Christmas had to be called off:

> One meal per day. Drink a lot of tea. Aldi is only place we go. Xmas is off. This is Covid Reality. Nine long months. What a joy to be self-employed!

CHANGE!
help!
Please!
AFRAID!
WE NEED
INCOME
security
WHAT ABOUT US?

Andrea had a similar experience, her diary entry closely echoing Che's:

> Food, heat and electric come 1st. They are essential. Presents are NOT and that is the harsh reality and the Covid reality. SHOCKING.

With no money, financial capability was irrelevant. There was nothing in the pot. For these parents, Christmas was off.

Deck the halls with boughs of holly!

Putting up the tree is a landmark in the festive season, a sign that Christmas is coming and that celebrations have begun. In our household, over one bored weekend in early November, we put up fairy lights, our artificial tree and played Christmas music. Charlotte's family did similarly, to find some relief after a tough couple of weeks:

> With 2 weeks of my kids bored during our mini lockdown and lack of resources, decent TV and money we decided to put our christmas tree up. It was so much fun.

Meg and her son were also early – getting the house decorated and tidied, and finding real joy in doing so:

> We've been painting and decorating and to get the house a bit more in order before Christmas. So we've had actually quite a lot of fun doing that.

But, while a hint of Christmas magic came early for some, others had a more tempered approach. Erik's tree went up just in time – two days before Christmas. Despite his attempts to find some Christmas spirit, his description reflects a common experience, everything was tarnished by COVID:

> I have put up a Christmas tree and will try to make things as special as possible but I could never have imagined living through a time like this.

Thea's tree kicked up active reminders of her personal and social disability. She tried to get her tree down from the loft in late October, keen for some early Christmas spirit, but her disability prevented her from reaching it, while lockdown stopped her from securing help from a friend:

> Feeling a bit useless today. Having no feeling in one arm and hand, I struggle ... going into the loft ... My son wanted to put the Christmas tree up today and I thought, 'why not ... If it puts a little bit of excitement in his life during these testing times, I'm all up for it!' Butttttt ... I can't even get up the attic ... Would normally have someone help me ... but the lockdown rules aren't going to let me.

Food, like trees and decorations so central to Christmas traditions, was a source of joy but also anxiety. Reflecting the importance of festive food, the families taking part in Covid Realities told us a great deal about food preparations in the run-up to Christmas. Lexie summarised the fears of many families experiencing 'less eligibility' at first hand:

> Feeling anxious and worried that Christmas is going to be whitewash. The kids don't have a lot, I've not got any 'Christmas' food/treats in and to be honest my mental health is suffering. How do I make something out of nothing?

Some families faced additional logistical difficulties, exacerbated by disability and lockdown. Meg was disabled, shielding, and was unable to go to the shops. If she could not secure a Christmas delivery, then Christmas was cancelled. She was consequently up early on the day delivery slots were released, hammering 'refresh' on her browser to make sure she had a chance:

> Ta dah! Success! I managed to secure a Xmas delivery slot ... I've chucked in our Xmas dinner & checked out ... Phew! It's like being on a game show – fastest finger first & all that ... I am reminded of Richard

Dawkin's book, *The Selfish Gene* – it really is a race
to secure survival between those that are fast enough
& those that are not.

And Callie's extra challenge came in the shape of a half-broken
oven that she couldn't afford to fix, making a full Christmas
meal a challenge:

> For about 4 years the big bottom oven hasn't worked
> at all … I'm just getting a large chicken but it's going
> to be challenging to cook in one tiny little top oven
> space especially along with my other roast veg …
> Thank god I've no high expectations of myself.

The expense of maintenance showed in other family accounts
– the broken hob, the bust oven, the kitchen too small to cook
a family meal.

Ted felt pushed to the wire, but with no spare resources took
on debt to make his daughter's Christmas work:

> I put the turkey on my credit card to have a normal
> Xmas … and I also need a food bank at some point.
> I tore myself up stigmatising my own actions, what
> sort of world we live in now?

The stigma Ted describes is well documented in academic
research, with families often trying to avoid the stigma of using
food banks (see Chapter 1). Ted's decision reflects a common
struggle: whether to take on (stigmatised) debt and have some
additional choice or to embrace the limited choice and public
shame of seeking charitable support. Callie summarises:

> Whatever the oven and the food bank can give is
> what we will take this year. This year is like no other,
> so the best way to approach it is recognise the limits,
> accept them and have a great time regardless.

This was the case for family after family. With no spare budget
and inescapable debt, Aurora, like many others, relied entirely
on food aid:

We received the vouchers today for the period over Christmas ... We should receive a delivery of a food pack from a charity organised by the school next week ... This time I believe they will be sending a full Christmas dinner without the meat. We're fortunate enough to not have visited the food bank so far.

The ghost of Christmas present: Christmas in lockdown

But what of Christmas 2020? Not only a Christmas, but a Christmas in lockdown. During this Christmas, government policy would restrict whom you could meet, where and for how long. If, as the anthropologist Daniel Miller has argued, Christmas is really a modern festival of the family, then a Christmas without them would not really be Christmas at all.[6]

As it approached, my own family made plans. Using the permitted Christmas rules (which in England allowed us to gather as a group of six for Christmas Day only), we would get together at my parents' house. A chance for us all to see each other after so long. However, as December progressed, cases of the new Alpha (or 'Kent') variant of COVID-19 were rocketing, as were hospitalisations and deaths. On 19 December, the government announced that in England an additional, extra-secure tier would be added to the three existing tiers of lockdown. Tier 4 would begin at midnight in multiple areas, including in Surrey, where my parents live. Mindful that my son had not seen his much-loved Granny (our support bubble) in months, I bribed him with £10, put him in the car at bedtime and we drove the four hours to Surrey. There, I surreptitiously picked up some presents while he had a 30-minute sleepy cuddle with Granny and told her about the drive down. With the boot loaded, after half an hour we turned around for the four-hour drive home, leaving the county border about ten minutes before midnight, when new lockdown restrictions kicked in.

As we drove north again, I was acutely aware of how much this had been enabled by my access to various resources – to private transport, and the ability to afford petrol. Financial security, and the spare money for a trip at short notice, had made all this possible – but it could well have been otherwise.

Perhaps you recognise some of this account: a sudden opening (or closing) of possibilities; a sudden chance, lost or seized, to see family or friends one last time as the curtain came down.

The families taking part in Covid Realities offered their own reflections on lucky chances, as well as on the difficulty of deciding how to react to the changing shape of the pandemic and lockdown rules. For a handful, the changes made no difference because they already lived with their closest relatives. Danni thought she was 'very lucky. As a single parent key worker I am in an extended household with my parents so we are continuing our plans'. Nellie and her family faced no changes because – perhaps quite sensibly – they had never fully trusted government plans:

> We thought the Christmas bubbles were ridiculous so had decided to spend Christmas at home. Keeping the older people in our family safe was much more important to us ... We don't have to travel, and we can do everything our way.

Other families developed workarounds – meeting in a motorway car park, for example, for a brief, hug-free exchange of gifts.

More broadly, worlds became smaller as opportunities fell through, leaving people isolated and alone. Erik is a single dad; his teenage daughter would see no one – no friends, no family – compounding the isolation of poverty:

> This year ... is unlike any other [because] my daughter is now unable to see her friends or engage with local church groups ... Also ... she would normally go out with her Godmother which can now not happen.

On the big day itself, many parents managed to make a good day of it. Those who did so worked hard to focus on events, experiences and relationships as the most important elements of a 'good Christmas'. Victoria was helped by the range of events nearby, as well as the sense of occasion and community spirit which made the day a good one:

Our town did a Santa drive-by ... so we got all dressed up in our holiday best and took a torch. Waited in the cold for nearly an hour ... conveniently close to a huge muddy puddle in a patch of fun looking grass ... I hyped it up and I'd brought a torch with me, so kiddies and I took the long way home.

Family made the day for Howie and Paige, who spent it quiet and happy, in the company of loved ones. This was more than enough, Howie explained:

Because we often work as a team as a single parent family, we have been able to do the same over the past year with all of the challenges that we have had. Christmas was fine, uneventful and calm, which is what I wanted really (our historical Christmases were often not secure or nice) so I was just happy with no drama.

Paige felt the same – after months of worrying about the presents she could not afford and the preparation she had not done, Christmas was a good day:

What a different Christmas this has been. Living with my daughter so making Christmas dinner in her house ... Got all the timings wrong. Forgot to cook the cocktail sausages and sprouts. But I should be grateful we had food to cook and that we were all there and healthy.

It is clear there were some positive experiences in which families found ways through, often in the company of others. But what we must remember is that families were making the most of an extraordinarily difficult time. The intensive and very hard work of budgeting for and navigating Christmas placed parents under very real financial pressures and emotional strain; strains that then so very often impacted negatively on their mental health (discussed in Chapter 5).

There were also many families who faced very difficult Christmases, with COVID-19 preventing normal plans from going ahead. Christmas was not only close to the anniversary of Aurora's husband's death, it also felt particularly lonely this year, with the absence of parental company and mandatory self-isolation:

> This was the first Christmas Day spent alone as a family unit of 3 in as many years. Having had to decline Christmas dinner with my parents, who are vulnerable. As a solo parent I've been properly isolated for the last week whilst I await COVID test results due to a constant cough.

The COVID Christmas of 2020 was unlike any other, with many of us experiencing a day without any of the usual family get-togethers, noisy celebrations and long, long festive meals. For families in poverty, though, there were some notable (if very unwelcome) constants, most especially the continued struggle to find a way through the financial demands that Christmas creates.

'They didn't even ask for much ... and we couldn't do it, my heart hurt for them.' Tough celebrations

Christmas, of course, is not the only expensive time of year. Big business and advertisers have latched on to the value of celebration, and every opportunity can now come with a gift. Father's Day, Mothering Sunday, Easter cards, birthdays and Christmas all present opportunities to sell. A card and good wishes are not enough, the latest toy, the upgraded games console, the newest release, the branded mug, are increasingly obligatory parts of annual celebrations.

Some families resist this drive to consume with every celebration, but this is easier for those who have a real and meaningful choice. For the parents and carers in Covid Realities, their everyday hardship often left them nervous about simply getting through Christmas and birthdays, anxious to be able to buy something for their children and to make sure they had a special day. Parents and carers told us about the small, persistent pains of exclusion, of what being judged 'less eligible' meant. The pains of never having quite enough for daily existence, let alone the small rituals that mark the passing of a year or the growing of a life. Ted told us how

> [my daughter] lost another tooth this month. The last time I just printed the standard certificate I made on [the] PC with no pennies. I can't bear this I won't sleep tonight.

The problem wasn't the event, though. It was the need for money, the drive for extra cash in budgets that could barely cover food. Tooth fairies made a relatively small impact, but birthdays were bigger, and hit families every year. Lexie felt the pain sharply, having moved on to Universal Credit when her husband became redundant. Now she could no longer afford even small birthday requests:

> It's been horrific from one day to the next worrying if we will make it!! Through all this 3 of our sons had birthdays ... but with the redundancy and not a spare penny it was so different and sad seeing their faces ... What they wanted was only around £15 each and we couldn't do it, my heart hurt for them.

When presents were up against heating or eating – sometimes even school uniforms – they were a luxury that had to go.

At the same time as desperately trying to provide gifts for children on their birthday, parents did sometimes speak of finding a way to celebrate together in what were extraordinary and difficult times. For Georgie, it was a birthday video call with her children's grandfather, who 'couldn't take the filter off' and swore abundantly; but the connection was made and her delight was apparent. For Destiny, it was her family deciding to visit – and the chance to be together for the first time in months:

> Been feeling so grateful today. My sister and her partner are visiting from London and we managed to

celebrate my brother-in-law's 30th birthday! I didn't expect to see them until Christmas ... so it's been such a treat. 💕

In moments like these, parents were able to create special celebrations, but the work of doing so was emotionally and practically intensive. With this intensive work, and with supportive input from family and friends, parents managed to make celebratory occasions a glimmer of light in tough times.

Christmas: from present(s) to future?

This chapter has described the work of Christmas and other times of celebration: the sheer energy of planning, developing, building up to and delivering the big day. With so much attention given to Christmas (and the New Year), arriving in a bleak winter with no celebrations for a while can seem cold and hard. All the more so when budgets have been bust and last spare pennies drained for a few Christmas festivities, meaning there is almost nothing left to see out the month.

A sense of this came through in the diaries of parents. Just as previous hard Christmases had been poor preparation for a Christmas spent under COVID restrictions, for many families this Christmas was little more than a warning of tougher times to come. Connie explained:

> I'm feeling so ground down with negativity and helplessness that I can't look forward to 2021. The news just seems overwhelmingly bleak. The kids are excited about Xmas and I have no doubt that it will be a lovely day for them but I genuinely worry about the weeks to follow ...!

Families knew that finances could be tough – where Christmas had stretched budgets, the start of the new year could well break them, as Howie said:

> I'm not shocked that we are in lockdown as I think I saw that coming. It does mean that I can't work,

so financially everything is unknown again, right after Christmas when finances are often a bit sketchy.

Finally, a handful of families reflected on the difficult social times ahead. Lockdown had now ground on for almost a year – what would be the cost to children if this was extended for another year?

> We survived Christmas financially and it was a good Christmas too. But … I think the next year will be quite telling – if we do not come out of Lockdown soon, if restrictions are not lifted so we can go back to cinemas, gyms, etc then I do not know what effect this will have on my girls. I want to remain positive, to look forward to a time we can look back at this and think we all came through together, but it's difficult to do that right now.
>
> Syeda

Christmas was over, but winter was still coming, and with it more lockdowns and a cumulative toll on parents' and carers' mental health.

Chapter five
**Winter lockdown:
hard times get harder still**

Led by Katie

At home in winter living on low income is one of the worst experiences I have had to go through, knowing that my daughter is warmer at school than at home and watching her shiver while trying to concentrate on homework. Our home sometimes becomes so cold that it is warmer outside. I actually walk to the local shop just to feel some warmth on my body, even though to do so makes me feel even more inadequate as I do not have enough money to go home with a small treat. The blankets we wrap ourselves in are acquired from a local Freecycle group. I just don't know how long I can keep this up, my daughter deserves better but I'm all she has. I know she appreciates what I can do, but I never feel that I'm able to do enough to keep her safe, healthy and able to face her own future with enough confidence and belief in a fairer world to be able to succeed to the best of her ability.

Brian

My mental health has taken the biggest knock ever, how can I tell my children 'Everything is ok'? I am angry with the government, the coldness of the season, being stuck in this house. I am told I must be a parent, teacher, doctor, carer and must be happy all the time for my family. I struggle to see a way forward.

Joseph

I felt so much anger and despair. The darkness in my head was overwhelming and I struggled to cope with my own worries along with everyone else's. The weight of the world on my shoulders. Living in my head is worse than living with your enemy.

Emma

The third national lockdown, which hit England and Scotland on 4 January 2021, came as little surprise. By the time it was finally announced, Wales and Northern Ireland were already living under restrictions. Rolling news coverage on the spread of the Alpha variant, a death toll of over 70,000, alongside blockades at Dover and cancelled flights as more than 40 countries closed their borders to the UK[1] meant that it was increasingly clear what was about to happen.

Still, though, families experienced uncertainties. Children in England returned to school for just one day, a senseless decision that left many reeling. As the lockdown news hit, parents and carers were unclear about how free school meal provision would be adapted at such short notice, and this time there was no end date in sight. For many who had faced localised as well as national restrictions, lockdown after lockdown after lockdown was becoming the new normal.

In England, the Westminster Government announced a roadmap on 22 February 2021, which aimed to end all restrictions by 21 June 2021. The roadmap was the government's attempt to provide some clarity about when and how restrictions would end. But there was little clarity for families on a low income, many of whom were still furloughed or receiving the temporary £20 uplift to Universal Credit, and who experienced considerable financial uncertainties (and often anxiety) in the run up to the March 2021 Budget. For how long would the top-up continue? And when would furlough end? Would any changes be gradual, or a sudden cliff edge? This gave those cold and dark winter nights of January a particularly ominous feel for those living in poverty, who waited nervously to see what decisions their political leaders would make.

Doreen Lawrence, mother of Stephen Lawrence who was murdered in a racially motivated attack in 1993, has used the term 'institutional indifference' to describe the treatment of social housing tenants in relation to the Grenfell Tower collapse and more broadly, especially in terms of race and social class.[2] Before the pandemic, Ruth Lister[3] argued that the term has a wider relevance, drawing comparisons between the 'hostile environments' created by both immigration and social security policy. In particular, she uses it to describe the design and implementation of Universal Credit. During the pandemic, the government's failure to provide reassurance to families about furlough, and about Universal Credit, further underlines its 'institutional indifference' to the everyday realities of poverty.

It is against this backdrop of winter nights and continued financial uncertainty that this chapter reflects on the mental health impacts of the COVID-19 pandemic on families living on low incomes, and on how the acute fears and anxieties of the first lockdown gave way to chronic stresses and strains over time. We will talk about how the relationship between poverty and mental ill-health was already ingrained in our society before the pandemic and how COVID-19 has made a difficult situation even worse. We will also talk about hope – how we have coped through these difficult and unprecedented times and what the future could look like.

Mental health before the pandemic

About a quarter of adults in the UK experience a mental health problem each year and it is often said that any one of us could be affected. To a certain extent this is true – after all, no one knows what is around the corner in life. Circumstances, as well as biology, can impact us in all sorts of ways. This suggestion of randomness, of 'any one in four', is useful for reducing the stigma and blame that has often been attached to experiencing a mental health problem. But we see that it is not all that helpful as soon as we dig further into the statistics about mental health. Some of us are much more likely to experience a mental health problem than others.

Poverty and financial insecurity put people at a much greater risk of mental ill-health. Trying to make ends meet is stressful, and it leads to other problems like debt and food insecurity that also negatively affect mental health. In fact, adults and children in the most deprived households in the UK are over twice as likely to develop mental health problems as those with the highest incomes.[4] Poverty is also stigmatising (as we discuss in Chapters 4 and 6), and it excludes, making it more difficult for people to take part in the types of social and community activities that promote well-being.

Changes to the social security system have also impacted negatively on mental health. Political and media characterisations of claimants as work-shy and undeserving of financial support leave people feeling misunderstood, undervalued and stigmatised. Earlier in the book, we explored the impact of stigma on people's uptake of support, their reluctance to access food aid when they needed it and their decisions to leave some financial support unclaimed. Stigma has a powerful impact on mental health too, affecting our self-worth and self-esteem. Added to this are the stresses of moving through the system itself. Changes to some benefits assessment processes have been linked with rises in anti-depressant prescriptions and suicides,[5] while the roll-out of Universal Credit in local areas has been linked with increased psychological distress.[6]

Compounding the issue, inadequate social security payments push households further into poverty in ways that are almost inevitably harmful to mental health. Taken against the broader economic backdrop of rising living costs and the growth in more precarious forms of employment, it is no surprise that families have felt under pressure. These changes have been fast paced: in 2010, around 168,000 people were employed on zero-hours contracts in the UK, but by 2018 this figure was well over three-quarters of a million.[7] Living in uncertain and insecure financial circumstances, as well as poverty, all takes a toll on mental health.

A perfect storm

With the number of people reporting mental health problems on the rise[8] even before the pandemic began, and made worse by the circumstances that unfolded in 2020, it is fair to say that as a nation we went into 2021, and the January lockdown, firmly on the back foot in terms of our emotional well-being. Families with children were further at risk once the pandemic took hold. As we saw in Chapters 2 and 3, rising living costs associated with being confined to homes, and inadequate financial support, plunged families who were already in precarious financial situations into further debt and arrears.

Alongside the broader impact of rising costs on already stretched budgets, some families taking part in Covid Realities experienced income shocks directly as a result of the pandemic (see Chapter 1). This left those living on low incomes having to juggle their fears and worries about the virus itself with uncertainty about how they would manage financially through a frightening time. It hasn't taken long for data to emerge showing that those who were worst off financially before the pandemic have experienced worse mental health during COVID-19.[9]

Many of the families taking part in Covid Realities regularly spoke of deteriorating mental health, and, perhaps unsurprisingly, the pandemic took a growing toll on mental health over time. For Destiny, it was the relentlessness of control measures and the persistence of the virus that ground her down:

> Been in a bad place mentally recently with the second wave evidently hitting the UK and the new restrictions that have been placed. It's such a mixture of emotion: I'm so upset that this virus is ripping through the country again; I'm angry that many still do not socially distance and such; I'm confused at what we can truly do to live a normal life; I'm scared that this is our new reality ... the list goes on. I put a brave face on for the sake of my daughter, but the truth is I'm actually just so fed up of the mixture of emotions COVID-19 has also brought.

By March 2021, mental health featured in around a third of all diary entries, most often anxiety, stress and low mood. These mental health effects were signs that people were feeling ground down over month after month of lockdown and uncertainty and enduring (and often worsening) financial hardship. To understand these negative mental health effects, we need to go back to the beginnings of the pandemic and remember how it affected us all.

The 'what ifs?' Pandemic pressures on mental health

> Lockdown has a habit of getting the mind into repetitive 'what if' narratives. What if we catch the virus? What if I get ill, who cares for my kids then?

What if they get ill, will I be able to care for them? What if the virus never leaves, what if lockdown lasts years, what if they never find a vaccine, what if what if what if? It's exhausting. And can easily lead one's mind down a dark rabbit hole of despair and fear.

Victoria

The pervasive sense of fear and uncertainty in those first few months of the pandemic will no doubt be etched into the minds of all of us for some time to come. One of the only constants was a daily government press conference sharing an increasingly bleak picture of hospital admissions and deaths. Dottie captures what this felt like:

Seeing the news makes me so anxious. It feels like a really scary rollercoaster.

Stressful daily dilemmas arose – do you watch the harrowing news coverage in the hope that today might be better than yesterday, or stay away from the media but risk missing an important update? Do you try to maintain a normal routine, or accept that any sense of normality has gone out of the window? Do you risk going out to buy essentials, knowing that when you return you could be carrying the virus?

With no vaccine on the horizon, and (initially) very limited treatment options, a return to normality looked ever more distant. Efforts to curb the virus seemed futile and all we could do was clap every Thursday night and wait, hoping the NHS would weather the incoming storm and that our collective efforts would minimise the number of lives lost.

As we saw in earlier chapters, for families living on a low income, there were additional pressures rooted in financial uncertainty. Questions surrounding the continued availability of support such as free school meals provision caused stress and anxiety, as did worries about managing the food, energy, schooling and entertainment costs associated with stay-at-home rules. As Zara and Dotty explain, for the parents and carers we spoke to, COVID-19 had frequently made a precarious and already distressing situation even worse for their mental health:

I am constantly fighting with myself to keep my depression on an even keel mainly due to my financial situation and the constant battles I face being with employment and ever-changing income, outgoings and benefit system as a single parent. I have to remain positive, or I would drown.

Zara

Unfortunately, our months have become filled with stress & anxiety on how to financially survive a month.

Dotty

Fear and anxieties about the future were certainly present in summer 2020, yet the sense of permanency or relentlessness that came later in the year had not fully set in. There was, though, a sense of loss among parents and carers of the day-to-day things that had quickly been taken away and seemed a long way from returning. Looking back, no doubt many of us can identify here with Connie:

I'm missing the small pleasures I love – cups of tea with friends, hugs, play dates with friends and their kids, sleepovers with my nephews.

'Strange times and not permanent'

Initially, there was hope that the first set of restrictions would work and that normal life would resume before too long. And while the first lockdown represented a huge adjustment, the warm weather provided opportunities to take advantage of walks and activities outdoors that helped to improve well-being. It provided families with a space to reconnect with children and – despite the daily pressures – be together. As Melissa told us:

These are strange times and not permanent, and there are also lovely times with the kids just enjoying walks in nature and bike rides.

Did you find yourself going outside more during that first summer of 2020, or were you already a fan of the great outdoors? Studies show that green space and getting out in nature is great for our well-being, not only because it usually means we are exercising – also good for our mental health – but because it provides time out from busy lives and a chance to reflect. In fact, people who spend more than two hours a week in nature consistently report higher levels of health and well-being than those who don't.[10] The importance of outdoor space became significant during periods of lockdown, in the context of long days and weeks spent at home. A survey by the Office for National Statistics showed that we exercised more as a nation, and the number of people spending time outdoors during the first lockdown increased by more than a third, as compared to before the pandemic – visits to the Royal Society for the Protection of Birds website, too, jumped by almost 70% during this time and there were increases in visits to parks and green spaces in almost every part of the UK.[11]

This increase was felt more in some places than others, and it did carry with it extra anxieties about virus transmission. As the newspapers and social media filled with images of packed beaches and parks, families worried about what this meant for their risk of catching COVID-19, as Nellie explains:

> The playgrounds shut, and all our usual haunts got really really busy. I hated it. Finding somewhere outdoors away from other people was impossible. As the pandemic went on we found that places are still really busy, which puts us off. In addition all the hospitality venues are closed so there are no toilets or baby changing facilities. This means we can't be out for very long at all. I think in general people are accessing outdoors more, but that is actually having a negative impact on my family.

As city dwellers, my[12] husband and I had little interest in the green spaces around us before COVID – the idea of walking for pleasure mainly conjured up images of lashing rain, blisters and soggy sandwiches! That is, until, with limited outdoor space at home, we decided to venture out for our daily hour of exercise. It was an odd time. The City of York, where we live, usually bustling with life and packed with people from all over the world at any time of year, was quiet and eerie – as if the city had lost its purpose. Monuments, tourist attractions and the multitude of businesses supporting the booming tourism in the city stood empty and closed. Our own business, a public house, had, as the landlord himself pointed out, never before closed its doors to the public – not even during two world wars. Yet now it stood silent, the laughter and warmth that usually rang out from inside, gone. Sad at seeing the city in this state, we dusted off our wellies and decided to see what green spaces we could find instead. We soon discovered fields and new places to amble, finding that fresh air and a walk were a real solace from days filled with Zoom and monotony, a great stress buster that invariably improved our mood. Lockdown made us converts to the benefits of the great outdoors. We were lucky that we had this option available to us.

The national appreciation for the outdoors was great to see, but as we collectively enjoyed improving our well-being through nature, inequalities in access to parks and green space were also evident. Research shows that those who may benefit the most from green spaces to improve well-being – people who are living on low incomes and therefore at greater risk of mental health difficulties – may be those who are least able to access them.[13] And, as summer turned into winter, reconnecting with the outdoors became less of a panacea for the stresses and strains brought about and exacerbated by the pandemic.

'Feels like I'm constantly worrying': dark days and long nights

Winter and the new lockdowns it brought with it left people struggling. For Riya, a Bangladeshi asylum seeker, the weather, virus and isolation combined to make for a pretty miserable situation:

> During Covid-19 the first time I passed my time with my children. That time I was happy and in summer-

time I could go outside with my children and we enjoyed that very much. Now we can't go anywhere because of the cold and the virus is increasing day by day. No friends can come to my house because of Covid 19. Now I'm waiting for vaccines because then we will be safe from the virus.

These strange times did begin to feel more permanent once winter took hold as we waited, and waited, and waited for the virus to be wrestled under control. Cold, wet days left limited options for family activities, especially with daylight gone by the time schooling had finished, and the relentlessness of just trying to get by was compounded by additional energy costs. Paige talks here about the profound stress caused by the stark and unimaginably difficult 'heat or eat' choices her family faced:

It's starting to get really cold now, so I'm worried about trying to heat the place as well as buy food. Should I do a quick blast of the fire or put the heat on for an hour? What will work out cheaper? Feels like I'm constantly worrying. Always choking with anxiety that I can't seem to control.

It is little surprise, then, that the intense anxiety and worries during the immediacy of the first lockdown gave way to sustained low mood, anxiety and reduced mental well-being as time went on, as Connie and Victoria explain:

I'm still functioning but I'm feeling so ground down with negativity and helplessness that I can't look forward to 2021 at the moment. The news just seems overwhelmingly bleak.

Connie

January is gonna be a dark, emotionally, month. The aftermath of Christmas, less money, sugar withdrawn children and the false hope that this vaccine news is bringing (so many messages about how January will be so different from Dec[ember], so many people don't seem to realise the vaccine will take months to be effective, nothing changing anytime soon). January is likely gonna be a tough month. I want to prepare but I just can't afford to do much more than I'm currently doing. Just so emotionally worn out. Can't wait for this year to be over. So scared what next year will bring.

Victoria

When we find ourselves in an acutely stressful situation, adrenaline kicks in – our heart rate increases and we become hypervigilant to the environment around us. This 'fight-or-flight' response comes from our caveman days, where encountering dangers such as predators meant quickly deciding either to stay and fight or to run away. It was a helpful response in the Stone Age, designed to ensure the body reacted quickly and effectively to perceived threats, and definitely a good idea when a sabre-toothed tiger is involved! We carry with us this evolutionary trait and, in some circumstances, particularly where physical danger is involved, it is still important for us today. Mostly though, it is not quite so useful for our modern times because the threats we often face are less about physical danger (in the UK at least) and more about our life circumstances.

When the pandemic took hold, many of us probably felt restless and struggled to sleep, unable to stop thinking about COVID-19 despite our best efforts at distraction. Did you find yourself on high alert all the time, or feel irritable and unable to unwind? These are all perfectly understandable reactions in the face of a highly transmissible and potentially deadly virus, as well as the significant upheavals and adjustments to everyday life that most people experienced.

Fight-or-flight reactions in the very short term are not necessarily harmful, but if this stress response continues for prolonged periods it is a different story. Studies tell us long-term or 'chronic' stress has negative impacts in many different ways. It can affect, to name only a few, our heart and circulatory system, our digestive system, our kidneys and our mood. It can give us headaches, muscle tension and poor sleep. It can make us feel anxious and low, sometimes leading to depression.

The research discussed earlier in this chapter shows that living on a low income coming into the pandemic has been linked with poorer mental health during the pandemic. When we looked through Covid Realities diaries across the year (July 2020–July 2021) specifically for references people made to their mental health, by far the biggest number related to experiences of stress and anxiety. When you add together the inadequacy of financial support before COVID-19, which then became intensified by the relentless worries of the pandemic, it is clear that parents and carers became at risk of experiencing chronic stress, with all the potential health implications described above. Diary entries from the winter months capture a feeling of tiredness, and of being burned out, as Nellie told us:

> I feel in a state of low level panic constantly, it's almost become normal. Trying to think about the future, finances and business plans it's so difficult. My anxiety is in overdrive and it's made me angry at a lot of things, situations, decisions and people, which I don't like feeling.

Howie described how this seemed to be impacting on everyone around her, too:

> I think I have noticed a general downturn in mood with people. It seems that this latest lockdown although not as lengthy as the last is having a significant effect psychologically. Before, I think people were managing to find ways through and to stay positive, but I am aware of people around me who are noticeably beginning to really struggle. They are tired, stressed and the future is uncertain.

'We all have cabin fever setting in'

No doubt many of us started to feel our mood dip over winter too, and especially during the January lockdown. It was a time when there were limited celebrations to look forward to – only post-Christmas bills to contend with – and a grinding sense of monotony, of Groundhog Day, set in. Fiona told us how difficult this was:

> I've spent this morning feeling low since waking up. There doesn't seem to be any hope in the air about when things will normalise again. I started taking a sleeping medication yesterday to help calm my anxiety. I have constant thoughts like when will we feel more free? Nothing feels in our control anymore.

Parents and carers muddled through, doing their best to spin many plates simultaneously, but a feeling of being cooped up and trapped at home with every day the same began to prevail, as Lexie captures here:

> It's cold, it's wet, it's winter! Not only is it winter but it's a lockdown winter. I'm trying to keep my mind together whilst trying to teach 4 kids in different age groups things I'm not even sure I understand anymore! They can't go out to play as the weather is atrocious!! We all have cabin fever setting in.

A survey by the Office for National Statistics undertaken from January to March 2021 found rising levels of depression, especially among those with the lowest incomes,[14] perhaps a reflection of the accumulation of stress upon stress upon stress brought about by the pandemic. Over time, hopelessness began to bite.

To cope with staring at the same four walls for the best part of a year, the nation took on hobbies, bought new TV subscriptions and went online shopping. Around 3.2 million of us got a new pet.[15] All of these things need money, though. Such attempts to provide solace from experiences of boredom, stress and low mood were very rarely available options for families living on a low income. For Victoria, a desire for a long nap reflected a longing to just put all the stresses and strains away – to sleep away the pandemic until better times:

> So sleepy, just constantly sleepy lately. I don't wanna clean anymore, or cook, or stress or paint or anything,

just really wish I could have a nice long nap. Like for a few weeks maybe, that would be nice. Maybe wake up and find our country isn't such a mess.

Meanwhile, we were bombarded with stories of self-improvement, of how we should use this time at home to lose weight, learn how to bake, or crochet, or meditate. I completed no less than five cross-stitch patterns during one lockdown that, much to the amusement of my husband, are (as he predicted) now sitting in a drawer. In the midst of everything though, sometimes it felt as though we forgot that with all the countless stresses and strains, it should have been enough just to get through the day.

Keep calm and carry on?

Typing the word 'stress' into Google brings back over a billion hits, and there are thousands of books, websites and experts telling us how to cope with it. The advice is seemingly endless, and the well-being industry is certainly big business. What helps you when you feel stressed out? Maybe you relax in a hot bath, talk to family and friends or spend some time in nature.

What if your financial circumstances made it harder for you to do any of this? If you live in an area with limited green spaces (as we found out earlier, more likely if you have a low income), and a hot bath or a comforting phone call is just too costly when your budget is already stretched to the limit? What do you do then? What if no amount of what we often hear described as 'self-care' will stop the money leaving your bank account to pay the bills much faster than it is coming in? If your debts are racking up and you struggle to feed your family, and there is no way to make it better?

We're often told that personal resilience is the key to managing stress, and never more so than over that year, when the phrase 'Blitz spirit' was evoked countless times by politicians and the media. There is no doubt that it is helpful to have coping strategies for difficult times, but the risk in championing personal resilience is that when people do struggle with their mental health the blame is laid squarely at their feet. The message that goes out (albeit implicitly) is that they simply need to learn better ways to manage with whatever is going on in their life, to pull themselves together and get on with it.

In my previous work as a community mental health nurse, I watched as financial circumstances brought person after person through the door in distress, sometimes in crisis. Problems with the benefits system, housing, with just not having enough money to live on. We tried to help where we could, but, as those readers who have used these systems will know, it is often a slow process. In this context, our clinical interventions – medication, therapies, coping strategies, mindfulness – felt at best like a sticking plaster, at worst irrelevant.

We have already seen in this book the ways in which financial adversity is harmful to mental health, and how this puts us at greater risk of mental health problems – a risk exacerbated by the pandemic. We have also seen that the social security system is not currently providing adequate support for families with dependent children, or indeed for anyone. We need to ask ourselves if it is appropriate, then, to ask people to be 'resilient' in the face of the inequalities and financial hardship that are causing the mental health problems in the first place.

Aurora put it like this:

> Started an online course to improve my mental well-being. To be completely honest – being taken out of poverty would be the biggest burden lifted already.

If, instead of focusing our efforts on creating better resilience, we addressed the root causes of poverty, we would go a long way to preventing the stress – and associated physical and mental health implications – which so many families on a low-income experience. To do so needs greater recognition of the role that financial circumstances play in our mental health, particularly for people faced with financial precarity and insecurity, and where financial support just isn't enough to meet basic needs.

A series of high-profile celebrity campaigns over the past 15 years have encouraged us to be more open about our mental health and to break down the stigma around mental health problems. While raising awareness in this way is welcome, this

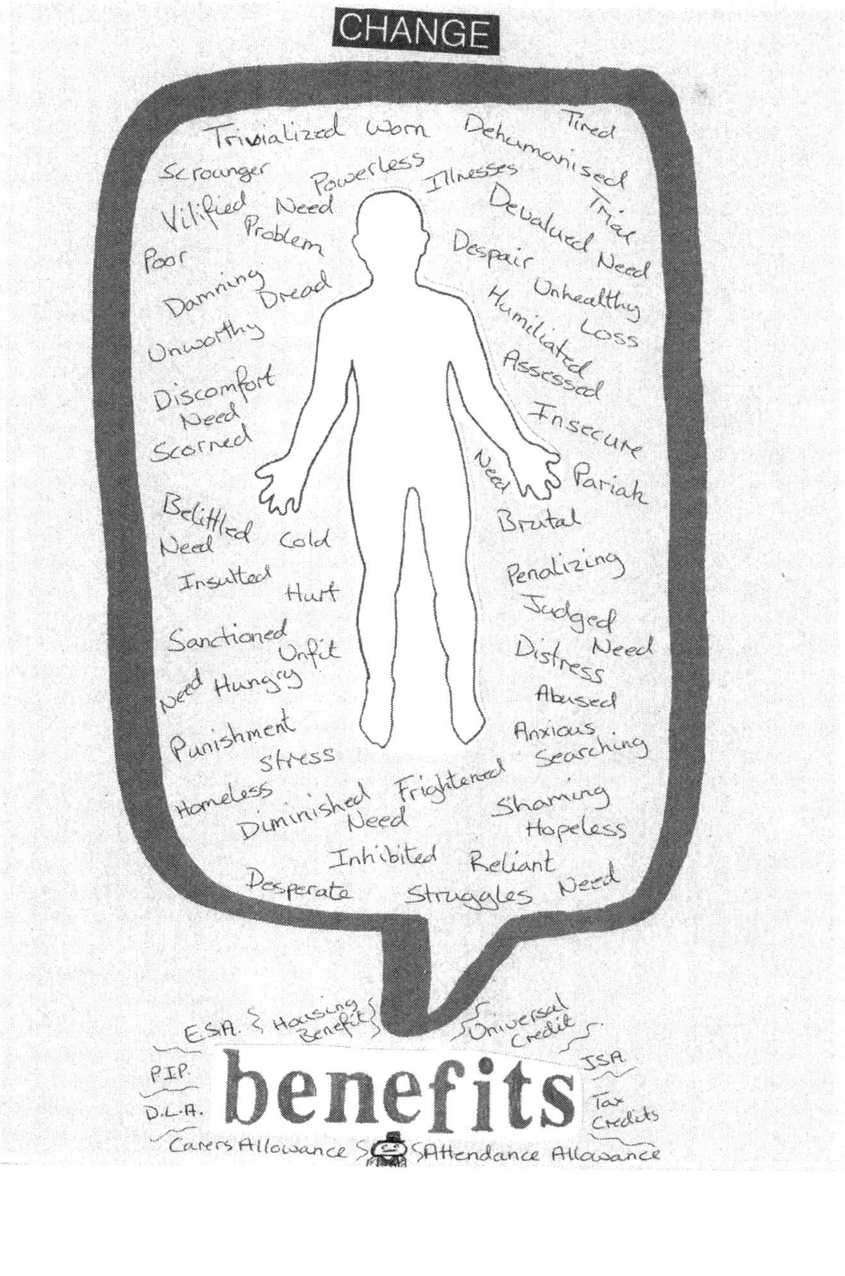
CHANGE
Trivialized
Worn
Dehumanised
Tired
Scrounger
Powerless
Illnesses
Vilified
Need
Devalued
Problem
Poor
Despair
Need
Damning
Dread
Unhealthy
Humiliated
Loss
Unworthy
Assessed
Discomfort
Need
Insecure
Scorned
Need
Pariah
Belittled
Brutal
Need
Cold
Insulted
Penalizing
Hurt
Judged
Sanctioned
Need
Unfit
Distress
Need
Hungry
Abused
Punishment
Anxious
Searching
Stress
Homeless
Frightened
Shaming
Diminished
Need
Hopeless
Inhibited
Reliant
Desperate
Struggles
Need
E.S.A.
Housing Benefit
Universal Credit
P.I.P.
benefits
JSA
D.L.A.
Tax Credits
Carers Allowance
Attendance Allowance

approach can only ever be a partial fix when we are not talking about the political, social and economic problems that produce both mental distress and stigma in the first place.[16]

'We spend all day every day at home alone'

Single parents are especially vulnerable to poverty, and also faced real risks to their mental health during the pandemic and repeated lockdowns. For solo parents and carers, who make up nearly three-quarters of Covid Realities participants, continued restrictions meant that limited social support – including from relatives and friends who would ordinarily help to share childcare and who provided meals as well as opportunities for social interactions – led to parents and carers feeling increasingly lonely as time went by, as Callie told us:

> I'm so lonely, chatting to my friends and family online is all I have for company. I have far too many essential outgoings and far too little money coming in. I'm so anxious and depressed, I've never felt this bad. I was put on anti-depressants last week by my GP over all the stress and worries I have over feeding and clothing my children and keeping the heating and lights on.

Callie's quote captures how isolating this time could be for parents and carers, particularly those without ready access to a support network, and in turn how difficult circumstances impacted significantly on mood. The loneliness that many experienced was further compounded for mothers of babies born during the pandemic, who were unable to celebrate new arrivals with family and friends, or to rely on their help with the demands of a new child. This was felt acutely by those affected, as Debs, a single mother with a history of mental health problems, set out in a blog piece for Covid Realities. Debs wrote:

> This took longer than I thought it would for me to write everything as my 9-month-old daughter was

crying non-stop as she saw all my attention was not really drawn to her 100% ... She is a lockdown baby who only knows mommy and strangers who wear masks. When we are around new people, she cries a lot and clings to me – I mean, who can blame her? She is not used to being social. Being a single mom to her sure has some good points – the bond we have with each other is really strong ...! But sometimes we all need that two minutes to ourselves, alone as adults, and I find it very hard to get any 'me time'. As someone who suffers from depression and anxiety, having a baby in isolation was surely a disaster and it brought postnatal depression because I did not have the support that I was meant to get ... When my baby girl would cry a lot, I was losing my mind. I would get really angry. One time I almost felt angry towards her – I was really scared of myself, I had to call social workers on myself to get involved. It was a cry for help. So social services offered me a place for her in day care so that at least I can be able to get two minutes to myself. But that is obviously not working because of the lockdown. I don't have any other childcare or support. Going into lockdown has really not helped the situation as I cannot be seen by my mental health clinic or get visits from my Community Psychiatric Nurse.

In Debs' account, we see how her existing mental health problems were compounded by the circumstances of the pandemic, leaving her vulnerable and unable to access specialist support. She was left with little choice but to try to manage new parenthood and her health difficulties alone. This experience of arriving into new parenthood alone was profoundly isolating, as Pearl, who also became a mother during the pandemic, explained:

I gave birth in April [2020], you could say it was the middle of the pandemic, and for someone having their first baby it was scary enough to think you're about to give up looking after just yourself to be responsible for this whole other person. I was isolated. I think most people that are isolated crack because it's one of the leading causes of depression and other conditions. I was used to being independent and thankfully it didn't affect my mental health. I don't have family really apart from my sister who lives far away and my parents who are substance misusers. I don't speak to them.

Pearl moved into a refuge shortly after her baby's arrival, and was grateful for the input from a specialist support worker:

I had the support workers to buy things for me from shops after I had given them the money. I appreciated it so much. There were no delivery slots left, everyone was panicking taking them. It made me worried whether I'd be able to get my son milk. Even in the shops a lot of things were gone and food was a struggle at times.

The pandemic was an extraordinary time to become a parent, and placed almost immeasurable strains on those making what is a life-changing transition even in more ordinary times. These strains were only multiplied by the financial hardship that the parents taking part in Covid Realities were also having to manage, as both Debs and Pearl reflected:

As well as mental health, let's talk about supermarkets – everything is expensive. I hoped that the government could be considerate, to add a little bit of financial support to people who are living on low income. As an asylum seeker I am not able to claim benefits. My daughter and I have to live off just £37 a week.

Debs

I don't own a car and I never did then. I believe there should be driving lessons grants for some teen mums, it would be so much better to be able to travel to get food. Even now I walk with my pram for 20 minutes to get to Tesco and I leave not getting everything I need because I can't carry it all and if I tie it to the pram it will fall off.

Pearl

A more adequate and supportive social security system, and more generous support for those seeking asylum, would have eased at least some of the strain that parents like Debs and Pearl faced. But such support was notable only by its absence. It was partly frustration at this absence, and the hope that things might be different, which led parents to get involved in Covid Realities, connecting online and working together to generate ideas for change.

'It feels like a community': unexpected impacts of Covid Realities

A small consolation in terms of the lack of contact with family and friends during COVID-19 has been our ability to use technology to stay in touch. Many of us have developed new ways to communicate and maintain social connections. While this could never act as a substitute for face-to-face time with family, friends and support networks, online forms of communication – for those able to access them – have enabled people to maintain social connections and to build new friendship networks. School, university and (for some of us) work have been adapted to online formats. People from all generations learned to use Skype, WhatsApp and TikTok, and the number of daily Zoom users rose from 10 million in December 2019 to a staggering 200 million by March 2020.[17] The phrase 'you're on mute' became an unfortunate mantra for the year.

As well as a space for writing down and reflecting on experiences of the pandemic, Covid Realities created a place for parents and carers to connect and, in a small way, reduce some of this isolation. It also made use of the possibilities that come with online communication, enabling parents and carers from all parts of the UK to get together virtually, sharing experiences, offering peer support and empowering each other to fight for change.

Ruth Lister[18] has written about how everyday forms of action, including 'getting by', 'getting (back) at', 'getting out' and 'getting organised' can be important when thinking about how people living on a low income can get involved in seeking change for themselves and others. Taking part in Covid Realities and sharing experiences was a source of not only solidarity but also resistance, and represented a way for parents and carers to speak out against stigmatising narratives. Meg, a divorced mother of three who was receiving disability benefits, wrote about how she was 'getting organised' and 'getting back':

> As an accidental activist & anti-poverty campaigner since 2018, the opportunity to tell those in power how the pandemic is affecting already precarious lives & livelihoods [by taking part in Covid Realities] was far too good an opportunity to waste. It's important to me that we hold those that govern us to account. To potentially be able to influence Government policy towards being more equitable, compassionate is an exciting prospect. It gives my life meaning & purpose to campaign for those who feel unable to speak up for themselves, many of whom don't realise how shabbily they are being treated by the current & previous Governments. I don't do it for reward or recognition – just to try to make a difference. And in return I have gained a huge family of fellow participants with whom I feel much love & solidarity.

The social aspect of Covid Realities – essential to 'getting by' – was important to Lola, who had two children and worked part time:

> Covid Realities has become my life saver during this pandemic, it has allowed me to take myself away from my family unit and be something more than mum and wife, just for a few minutes I'm involved in something much bigger. It feels so important the work Covid Realities is doing and I'm so very thankful to be a part of it in every way I can be. I

love my family so much but it's also nice to be able to do something away from them and find myself again. Covid Realities has brought out my creative side which for many years I'd lost due to fitting into the wife and mum role completely. I forgot how creative I can be and how fun and therapeutic it is which has helped me no end in my dark times. This platform is also very valuable to me as I can discuss and 'put the world to rights' with like-minded people so I don't feel so alone and they understand what I'm going through too.

Alongside providing a space to get back and get organised, parents and carers told us this support was an important part of being involved in the project.

Isla described what she saw as the creation of a Covid Realities 'community':

It feels like a community. Hearing other people's life experiences and thoughts and opinions is helpful. Knowing other people are going through similar to you makes you feel like you are not alone. Knowing we're trying to make a difference between us to everyone's lives is also empowering! Together we are making a difference.

Coming together through monthly meetings, arts-based workshops and a range of other activities provided opportunities to meet, talk and collectively work together for change. In doing so, participants created connections and told us about the positive impact on their mental health. Lexie sets out how significant the benefits of involvement were for her:

Covid Realities has meant the world to me during what has been an incredibly difficult year. Covid Realities has helped my mental health in an insurmountable way and at times literally kept me sane, it has given me a place to express my worries and woes but it has also given me a place to share my little victories and has given me a purpose, I have become part of something for the better, I have become a voice in the fight for justice, fairness and for equality.

Elsewhere, others were also taking action and finding ways to respond positively to the pandemic. Indeed, since the start of the pandemic we've seen how pre-existing grassroots groups such as Poverty2Solutions and the APLE Collective have mobilised and responded to the challenges facing people on a low income, emphasising the importance of working together to put the voice of lived experiences at the heart of policy making. Thousands of new mutual aid groups have also sprung up in the UK since 2020, spurred on by the pandemic. There are now an estimated 4,300 such groups in the UK, with three million volunteers offering their support to people in their local community[19] (several Covid Realities parents delivered food aid in their own communities). This is itself a reason to be hopeful, but there are perhaps others too.

Reasons to be hopeful?

Although the winter brought further lockdowns, it did also bring some cause for cautious optimism. It was in England that the first-ever person in the world received a COVID-19 vaccination, with 90-year-old Margaret Keenan securing her place in the history books with a jab to her arm in December 2020. At this point in the pandemic, it was becoming clear that COVID-19 was here to stay for the foreseeable future, and vaccines were rightly hailed as the best route to easing restrictions.

The arrival and roll-out of vaccines was a hopeful moment and, while the prioritisation of older and clinically vulnerable people meant that vaccinations for most adults were still some time away, it was definitely good news all round. Destiny and Nellie sum up what this meant for Covid Realities participants and their families:

So the vaccine has been given to the first of so many in the UK and I'm feeling somewhat hopeful that this may be the first step to helping us gain some normality.

Destiny

I will be glad once my parents have had it because then we will be able to see them, and hug them, and they can help with childcare.

Nellie

By February 2021 over 500,000 people were receiving a vaccine every day.[20] The gradual lifting of restrictions, contextualised by a new, emerging variant of COVID-19, increased the urgency of the vaccine roll-out. Vaccine hesitancy and emerging inequalities in uptake created a divisive debate about the reasons behind the continued spread of the virus. The focus of this discussion centred on variations in vaccine take-up across different towns and cities, often naming explicitly those areas with low uptake. But, as Yasmin Qureshi, MP for Bolton South East, an area that became the epicentre of the debate because of its low take-up, pointed out, these narratives did not take into account inequalities in access to the vaccine, or factors associated with virus transmission more broadly.[21] Che explains how socioeconomic factors influenced how easily people could gain doses of the vaccine:

I cannot get an appointment for the vaccine as it's too far away, and we sold the car last year. Closest place is in another town! Makes me go off having it done the longer this goes on. Still broke and living meal to meal so no big changes really.

The nuances of the difficulties faced by people living on low incomes who were trying to gain access to the same opportunity for protection against the virus as everyone else but were prevented by financial circumstances were all too often missing from this discussion.

The easing of restrictions also brought about mixed emotions among parents and carers taking part in Covid Realities, visible from contrasting diary entries as shops and the hospitality industry reopened:

What an exciting day!!! For lots of people today is the day to start their normal daily lives again. I can't wait to pop to Primark to top up the kids' T-shirts and leggings! They have both grown so much in the last year!! Being able to spend some time in a pub garden with my beautiful family or friends. To regain a little social life. To be able to go outside on actual dates with my partner!! Take the kids to the farm, zoo, theme park!! To get back to work and work hard to provide a better life for my babies. I'm feeling so so positive today and am hoping that this was the last lockdown.

Lizzie

Hoping everybody is going to stay safe and sensible now more restrictions are being eased across the country. With the new variant spreading and not fully understood, I am getting extremely anxious about leaving home again and mixing with other people. I have had both my vaccines now but do not feel completely safe and protected. It's not over yet!

Erik

Nevertheless, the 'great unlocking' also frequently meant more of the same struggles in the context of financial insecurity and a continuation of the negative impacts on mental health of the past year. For some families, there was likely to be little change in their circumstances:

I have become apprehensive about the impending relaxation of lockdown. Until I'm able to find suitable employment our situation remains precarious. It has been constantly on my mind and a source of much anxiety. For many it will mean continuing as normal. For people like us the situation in a way remains unchanged. We are unable to afford to participate in normal society.

Aurora

> Today things began to open up more, but rather than feeling joy I am mentally exhausted. I have just paid monthly bills and don't have much left to go back out and enjoy the easing of lockdown.
>
> Fiona

As Aurora and Fiona write here, it seems that for many families a life returning to normal simply meant more of the same – more of the hardship, exclusion and stress associated with financial adversity. This set these families out of step with the national mood, and the national conversation, a reminder that being at the sharp end of socioeconomic inequalities matters, both because of a lack of money and because of its wider exclusionary consequences (see discussion in Chapter 2).

Looking ahead: 'We know what needs to be done. Let's do it.'

> So like the good British lass that I am, I'll stick on the kettle, a fresh smile and I'll just carry on carrying on. It's all I can do currently.
>
> Victoria

During the pandemic we have all learned more about our own ability to cope with the unknown, with hardships and the many different forms these can take. We have learned about our capacity, as Victoria puts it, to 'carry on carrying on' when life as we knew it was disappearing around us and new tragedies arose every day.

We have learned that getting outside really matters, and learned (or been reminded) of the importance of relationships with families and friends. And we have learned to be adaptable, moving online when we couldn't pop round to friends for a cuppa, finding new strategies in our efforts to cope with hard times.

But we need to exercise caution in how we think and talk about mental health. We must recognise that the UK population will likely emerge from the pandemic with worse mental health than before COVID-19, a situation that has been compounded by the acute and chronic stresses during the pandemic – particularly for families living on a low income. Elizabeth puts it like this:

> I think all the strain and stress of the lockdowns have put extra strain on an already full plate. I was struggling as a single parent, having escaped domestic violence. My parents are aged so we don't get much support so the only break I get from caring for three children, one of whom is autistic, is when they are at school. The lockdowns have been exhausting and have left me with physical health problems as well as worsening mental health, which will set me back months or maybe years from being able to get back to the work-place.

To account for the additional difficulties people have faced as a result of the pandemic, in 2021 the government announced an extra £500 million worth of funding for mental health, to be delivered through the Mental Health Recovery Action Plan.[22] This funding will be used to expand talking therapy provision and community mental health services, and will have an additional remit to 'level up' mental health and well-being through initiatives in more socioeconomically deprived areas to improve debt advice, careers support and loneliness.

Yet, while additional funding may be welcome, this plan arguably represents a resilience-focused, rather than a preventative, approach to improving mental health. Tackling the root causes of mental ill-health by improving socioeconomic inequalities could stop so many problems from arising in the first place, along with the untold distress they cause to individuals and families.

If there is one positive to emerge from COVID-19, it is that we are now having national discussions and debates about the impact of social inequalities on our health. The pandemic has laid bare the structural barriers and disadvantages faced in particular by people from racially minoritised backgrounds and people living in poverty – as we talked about in Chapter 3. It is imperative that we keep this momentum going if we are to have any hope of emerging from the pandemic in a better place than the one we started from.

Investment in a more caring social security system that provides adequate levels of payments and appropriately recognises the needs of families with children would be a good place to start. As academic and health inequalities commentator Sir Michael Marmot, who is working on ways we can 'build back better' and, crucially, fairer, has said:[23]

> 'Everyone should have at least the minimum income necessary for a healthy life. That means, ideally, all people of working age should be in work. That's the desirable state. And in work, they should be paid a living wage. If they can't work, for whatever reason, then the welfare system should be sufficiently generous for their health not to be damaged by that experience. We know what needs to be done. Let's do it.'

When we asked Covid Realities participants what they thought was the best way to improve their mental health, they unanimously agreed on where change was most urgently needed. Parents and carers told us that improving the social security system, its processes and how it interacts with those who use it would contribute the single, biggest improvement to their mental health. And that is where the conversation about improving our nation's mental health needs to begin.

The post-pandemic world represents a new opportunity to take the preventative action needed to improve both individual and public mental health. But, unless we address fundamental socioeconomic inequalities, mental health and well-being interventions can only ever be a partial fix for those experiencing financial hardship.

The next chapter takes us to the March 2021 Budget, when the government had an opportunity to address exactly these inequalities. We will sadly see, though, how this opportunity was squandered, with families in poverty being left instead to face the negative mental health effects of a toxic combination of financial hardship, endemic uncertainty and persistent, overlapping insecurities.

Chapter six
The Budget:
counting the money
we do not have

Led by Jim

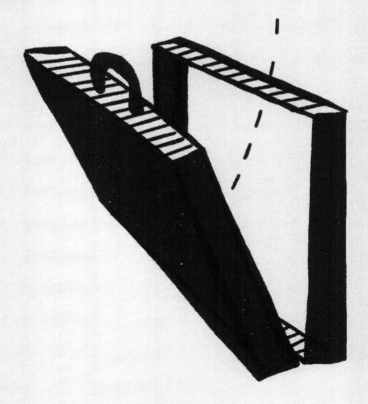

The Government did the right thing at the start by introducing £20 a week extra into households on Universal Credit, but they missed so many families out that were stuck in the benefit cap or on legacy benefits, they saw nothing extra to help them with additional costs. Removing the minimum income floor and introducing furlough support was much needed as well ... The five week wait at the start of an application for Universal Credit is too long and shows clearly that this government hasn't a clue about the reality. You can only exist for five weeks with no support if you have a large surplus of savings: many applying had nothing. They were driven into taking on government debts which reduces their level of support, thus creating a vacuum of constantly borrowing when you finish paying off the debt.

Caroline

An uplift of £20 per week was announced for those on Universal Credit. We find we're not eligible due to being capped.

Aurora

We are lost
I drink
She dies
We are lost

And quietly I count the money I do not have

Jo

The safety net

On Wednesday, 3 March 2021, Rishi Sunak delivered a keenly anticipated Budget, which would significantly affect the finances of many millions of households. Many participants in Covid Realities waited anxiously to see what Sunak would announce. Whether affected by the £20 increase to Universal Credit and Working Tax Credit, the Coronavirus Job Retention Scheme (CJRS, or 'furlough'), or the Self-Employment Income Support Scheme (SEISS), any changes would have profound and immediate consequences for their lives. Would the measures continue? Or were people going to see their incomes suddenly plummet?

A year earlier, and on the verge of the first lockdown, the Chancellor had introduced these measures in an emergency budget, delivering interventions on a massive scale. By the time it closed, the cost of furlough alone amounted to £70 billion.[1]

The Chancellor's package of support was introduced to 'protect people's jobs, offer more generous support to those who are without employment' and to 'strengthen the safety net for those who work for themselves, and help people who stay in their homes'.[2] At the time, and to great fanfare, Sunak described them as 'unprecedented in the history of the British state'. The kind of inflated political claim that might normally be regarded with some scepticism on this occasion attracted no noticeable disagreement. Everyone seemed surprised, stunned. Things that had seemed unimaginable only days before were quickly becoming the new normal – here was a Conservative Chancellor announcing a scheme to pay people 80% of their wages *not* to go to work.

Announcing these emergency measures at the start of the pandemic, Sunak used an everyday metaphor, describing his intention to 'strengthen the safety net'. This is a common phrase. We also speak of 'holes in the safety net' or 'fixing the safety net'. The image conjured is of workers at a height, constructing skyscrapers or cleaning windows. Or perhaps a trapeze artist, or a tight-rope walker, net safely positioned beneath them should they miss a hold or put a foot wrong.

In some ways this is a useful way of talking. Life often feels risky, and nobody wants to fall. It would be cruel – criminal even – to fatally tamper with someone's safety net. But in other respects this isn't always a helpful – or accurate – way of talking about social security. For one thing, all of us depend, to varying degrees, on forms of collective social support, often without realising it – and not just when we fall. The image of a safety net also casts the world in very simplistic, binary terms of success and failure. For most people life isn't really like that. It is a mix of both, with risks often precariously managed. Safety nets are there to protect us from individual difficulties – losing our footing – but the social security system often compensates for underlying economic problems, which are beyond an individual's control. It steps in when the market economy fails to adequately meet people's basic needs. It should also step in when misfortune strikes – bereavement, ill health, disability – all circumstances that can cause us to lose our balance.

The image of the safety net also positions the help we might receive as below us, as something we hope not to need. Yet, informal forms of help and support are often tightly intertwined with the most important relationships of our lives. And the social security system, too, is part of the fabric of life for many people – whether as Universal Credit, Child Benefit or, in broader terms, as the welfare state of schools, hospitals and GP surgeries. Such institutions play different roles for each of us, and can be more or less prominent in our lives, with their significance also changing at different points of the lifecourse (especially important, for example, when bringing up children or towards the end of our lives). Just like the NHS, then, social security is something for all of us, and, if delivered effectively and with adequate support, it can be seen as a feature of our welfare state infrastructure that is universal in its value and in its potential reach. This is not how social security is currently conceived of, though, nor how it is delivered.

Between eating and heating

In the event, in March 2021 the Chancellor extended both the furlough scheme and the £20 increase to Universal Credit for a further six months, until September 2021. This provided some temporary relief, while simultaneously starting the clock on another anxious countdown. Many had hoped for something more substantial or permanent.

By late 2019, unemployment benefits rates in the UK were among the lowest across all of the Organisation for Economic Co-operation and Development countries. As a proportion of average weekly earnings, unemployment benefits had fallen to their lowest level since the creation of the National Assistance Board in 1948.[3] The £20 increase to Universal Credit announced in March 2020 was the most significant and substantial increase that working-age benefits had seen in half a century.[4] Charlotte wrote about the increase, 'I know to a lot of people £20 seems like nothing but to me it is HUGE.'

Although certainly welcome, the £20 increase still did not go nearly far enough towards addressing the financial problems that low-income families faced. As we described in Chapter 1, families faced additional costs because of lockdown, and this flat payment did not adjust for need according to family size. A single person received exactly the same in additional support as a family with two adults and three children.

For those who were struggling in poverty before the pandemic, there were often essential purchases that had been postponed – children's clothes, broken appliances, unpaid bills – ready to quickly eat up the additional income that the Universal Credit increase brought. As Nellie wrote, 'It's helped in that we are less over our monthly budget. [But] it gets sucked into the deficit. It definitely helps, but we don't notice it as an actual extra £20 to spend.'

The £20 increase also exhibited many of the same divisive tendencies that had defined the austerity era. The increase wasn't given to everyone, only to claimants of Universal Credit and Working Tax Credits. Among those who didn't see any rise in their benefit income were people whose benefits were capped (discussed further below) and people claiming legacy benefits.[5] People claiming these legacy benefits were more likely to be disabled, ill or to have significant caring responsibilities. They were people like Meg, whom we first met in Chapter 2. Meg was a former nurse, disabled and claiming ESA. She did not receive the increase, but her additional needs meant her already insufficient income was further stretched during the pandemic. As she explained:

> The past 3 weeks, I have been self-isolating with my son, because I had spinal surgery on Monday 30th November & it was part of the pre-op prep. I'm home now, but because I'm in a lot of pain, I still can't go out much as yet & because I'm not allowed to drive for 6 weeks, if I need to go out for appointments etc., I have to take a taxi there & back, which is increasing my expenses. Additionally, I have to pay to have my shopping delivered now too, which adds another £3 minimum onto the charges. I am in receipt of legacy benefits, therefore have not benefited from the hopefully not-so-temporary £20 per week uprating to Universal Credit, which would help massively with these extra unexpected costs.

As Meg makes clear, the decision to temporarily raise benefit levels for some people was not based on any serious assessment of people's needs – if it had been, then people claiming legacy benefits would also have received the raise.

The public reason given for not extending the increase to legacy claimants was that the administration would be too complex. This is perhaps one way of saying that it was not a political priority. When, in June 2020, the House of Commons Work and Pensions Select Committee called on the government to extend the increase to claimants of legacy benefits, the Department for Work and Pensions' (DWP) response was to say that such claimants 'can make a claim for Universal Credit if they believe they will be better off'.[6] One conclusion that might be drawn is that the DWP intended to use the £20 increase, and the extraordinary circumstances of the pandemic, as a way to 'nudge' people from legacy benefits and onto Universal Credit. Another possible explanation could be what some researchers have called 'COVID exceptionalism' – the idea that the people claiming benefits because of the pandemic were different from other claimants, and deserved better treatment.[7]

In March 2021, Covid Realities helped to organise a meeting over Zoom between MPs and parents and carers on a low income. Most of those who attended seemed to agree that low benefit levels at the start of the pandemic had made swift action necessary: the 'safety net' needed strengthening. But this rapid decision to raise benefit levels also raised an important question. As Helen, one of the parents involved in Covid Realities, put it to the digitally assembled parliamentarians:

> 'I'd like people to think about why it was necessary to introduce a £20 uplift at the start of COVID: surely this is an acknowledgement in itself that the support given to low-income households just isn't enough for them to live on?'

Helen was asking the parliamentarians to honestly confront the logic of a policy which, as she pointed out, could only be seen as an admission that benefits were too low. And she was right. When policy makers have talked about this policy, they have indeed admitted that benefits are too low – although with a crucial caveat: too low for *some* people.

For example, when Sir David Freud, one of the architects of Universal Credit and a former DWP minister, called for the £20 increase to be made permanent, he did so on the basis that '[w]hen you've got lots of people who are *not normally* in the welfare system needing to subsist, the rates aren't good enough' [my emphasis].[8] Similarly, Neil Couling, a senior civil servant and Director General of Universal Credit, made the following admission when talking about how the raise came about:

> 'I wanted to help people affected by the pandemic and what I said was that meant I couldn't create a new class of benefit claimants pre-COVID and post-COVID on Universal Credit, so for want of a better phrase, there was a kind of windfall gain for existing Universal Credit claimants.'[9]

For both David Freud and Neil Couling, the problem was not so much that benefits were too low, but that they were going to be too low for *new claimants*. Although Couling said he wanted to avoid creating a new class of claimants, it was exactly such a distinction between new and existing claimants that seemed to underpin his thinking. The reasons for making this distinction are not spelled out, beyond the idea that, unlike new claimants, existing claimants were already accustomed to living on so little. The implication was that existing benefit levels were sufficient for those already accustomed to them – but not for anyone else.

Here, the accounts and explanations of policy makers perhaps raise more questions than they answer. For one thing, they contradict an extensive body of academic research into the experiences of people living on low incomes, which documents in detail the daily struggles that many face in simply getting by.[10]

A year after the increase was introduced, in the lead-up to the 2021 Budget, the Joseph Rowntree Foundation and other organisations launched the 'Keep the Lifeline' campaign, urging the government not to end the increase and instead to make it permanent. For many, the extra £20 was indeed a lifeline, but the difficult truth is that for others it simply slowed down the rate at which they were going under. While successive governments have been keen to underline people's personal responsibility for the circumstances they face, in practice, political choices and political actions have impoverished many, and led to an unprecedented drop in life expectancy for the most deprived groups.[11] If the £20 was a lifeline in turbulent waters, then it was also true that many of the politicians extending it had spent the previous decade pushing people into the water.

Nevertheless, for some Covid Realities participants the £20 increase was the difference between eating and going hungry. Danni, a nurse and mother of two, told us that 'I find it invaluable. It is half of my shopping budget for the week for me and my 2 kids.' For others, the £20 increase meant choices that they might not otherwise have had – although these were still difficult choices about which needs would go met and unmet. As Lexie, a mother of four, put it, 'The £20 is the bare minimum of help to be honest. I know that sounds ungrateful but £20 doesn't cover much these days. By the end of the month we are still choosing between eating and heating.'

The inadequacy of the social security response contrasts with the scope and scale of other COVID-19 policy measures. Through the furlough scheme, launched in April 2020, the government committed to paying 80% of people's wages, up to a maximum of £2,500 per month. By May 2020, 8.9 million jobs were furloughed (experiences of furlough are discussed in Chapter 1). The sectors that made the most use of furlough were retail and hospitality, but the scheme was open to anyone whose job couldn't be performed, or was at risk because of the pandemic.

The furlough scheme wasn't perfect. It was open to abuse by exploitative employers, and there were cases where companies claimed money for furlough but nonetheless pressured their employees to come into work. Nevertheless, the different way that people in work and people out of work were treated reflects a long-standing preference for targeting government support at 'hardworking families'.

For people able to access the furlough scheme, it provided a level of security that went far beyond anything provided by Universal Credit. Those who were placed on furlough spoke of their 'luck', recognising that having to claim Universal Credit would have been a much more difficult experience. However, although they were able to access a higher level of support, people on furlough still faced considerable uncertainty and, for some, financial difficulties. In this respect their experiences were similar to those of people claiming Universal Credit. Like people receiving the £20 increase, they were often left guessing what the government would do next – would the scheme end, or would it continue?

If, on the one hand, the government's social security interventions of March 2020 can be defined by their scope and scale, then it is also true that they were characterised by delay and indecision. This was a pattern that continued throughout the pandemic. Having introduced measures, the government often refused to say how long they would continue, in what form, or how they might end. Time and again, deadlines for ending support measures were extended, sometimes at the very last minute. This was a political decision that communicated the provisional, temporary nature of the measures. But keeping the emergency measures shrouded in uncertainty had an enormous impact. It was a decision that betrayed a brutal disregard for people living on low incomes. For those encountering this disregard for the first time – for new claimants during the pandemic – it could be a jarring and disconcerting experience. Ted was one such new claimant. When we asked what difference the £20 had made, and what it would mean if it were taken away, he wrote:

> Being new to Universal Credit I can't say I've noticed any change, but I will say this: if it was taken away it'll push families to the brink.

Enzo wrote about her worries concerning the March 2021 Budget:

> The wait to hear about the £20 increase is a bit daunting. I'm not getting enough money as it is and having an extra £80 [a month] taken is going to make my finances take a turn for the worst, seeing as the cost of living has basically doubled since the first lock down …

How to prove hardship?

The reassuring thing about safety nets is that they are always there, ready, anticipating and cushioning your fall. You don't need to apply for them, call any 'helplines' or prove your eligibility while falling. The same isn't true of social security benefits. For anyone with even a passing familiarity with the UK benefits system at the beginning of the 21st century, the DWP's response that people should apply for Universal Credit 'if they believe they will be better off' will seem cruelly disingenuous. Claiming benefits can be difficult, time-consuming and likely to involve delays and bureaucratic mistakes. People widely fear even small changes to their benefits, let alone the full transition to Universal Credit. Some legacy benefit claimants, including those receiving the severe disability premium, moved to Universal Credit and found themselves worse off.[12]

Howie is a self-employed single mum with three children. A former teacher, during the pandemic she worked as an education freelancer. She described being self-employed as 'feast or famine', always moving back and forth between times when 'you have work and cash but no time' and times when 'you have no work and cut back on everything but much more time for family'. Howie claimed Working Tax Credits (WTC), which supplemented her income from paid work. She was not keen to transfer to Universal Credit (UC), and this was a source of worry for her:

> There are … so many horror stories about UC that I fear any contact or communication about WTC, just in case I have to swap over. We could not survive 5 weeks without any WTC and that basically scares me into avoiding any contact at all even if it could potentially be in my favour.

Chief among Howie's concerns about transferring to Universal Credit was the five-week wait – often longer – before getting the first payment. Universal Credit is also typically paid monthly, whereas most legacy benefits are paid fortnightly. For many people, the transition to Universal Credit threatens to introduce unmanageable uncertainty into already uncertain lives, disrupting finely balanced budgets and everyday strategies for getting by. The five-week wait often leads to a domino effect of debt, mental health challenges and hardship for parents and their children.[13]

Universal Credit claimants waiting for their first payment can apply for an 'advance payment'. Advance payments are often for quite large sums of money, required to cover the long wait for a first benefit payment. This means that many people start their benefit claim already in debt, with their repayments further reducing an already low rate of benefit.

Notably, while the recovery of debt deductions from benefit payments was temporarily suspended at the start of the pandemic, the government never stopped recovering advance payments of Universal Credit. Around one million people who claimed benefits during the first wave of the coronavirus pandemic were having money regularly deducted from their payments. Debt deductions inevitably reduce a household's income, and make budgeting even harder.[14] In fact, around half of all families reported a new or worsened debt problem according to Child Poverty Action Group.[15] We can see how this played out for Victoria:

> I paid all my bills that month, including rent for five weeks, but after bills and needing to stock up on covid related purchases, not of bog roll, lol, but of hand sanitiser, disinfectant, children's medicines, etc (anyone else notice how scarce Calpol quickly became? – even basic adult paracetamol at our local shop went from 29p a pack to £1.68!). I ended up taking a credit card out (something I never wanted to do). And needed to take a loan from the only family member I have left (a toxic person who reminds me constantly how useless I am – which I'm not FYI).

Benefit levels are already too low to escape poverty, but when they are reduced further by deductions, this only pushes families further into the red, and further below the poverty line.

Transfers to Universal Credit can be triggered by any change of circumstance – something that people are not always aware of. This is what happened to Ted, a single father. In his own words, Ted is 'very stubborn' and doesn't like 'asking for help in case this reflects on people's views of my ability to care for [my] daughter. I have always been a provider, an old-fashioned type.' Before the pandemic, Ted had been self-employed in property maintenance, working part-time during school hours. Working Tax Credits and Child Tax Credits topped up his income.

When lockdown was announced and he could no longer work, Ted wrote, 'boy was my worries through [the] roof. Days I spent ringing Universal credit, stress at max.' During those first weeks of lockdown Ted heard that self-employed people unable to work should apply for Universal Credit. In a state of panic, Ted followed the available advice, and called the Universal Credit telephone line. In doing so, he unknowingly ended his claim for Working Tax Credits and Child Tax Credits, and initiated his transfer onto Universal Credit, making himself worse off in the process.

On that first occasion, when Ted finally got through to speak to someone, he described how they

> offered me £500 advance. Immediately my anxiety kicked in, I was retching almost sick whilst on [the] phone. The fear of taking money to pay back with not knowing of future finances. However, days later I noticed my working tax and child tax credits had stopped. Again my anxiety kicked in. After a phone call with a Citizens Advice woman who rang me, she said they would stop. No one had told me this. She said ring them [DWP] back [and] get another £500, you will need it. Total £1000 advance paid back at £80 per month. This doesn't hit you till you can't get through the month.

Very quickly, during a period of intense stress, Ted had upended his carefully balanced finances by calling the Universal Credit line. Rather than clarify and stabilise his situation, this act introduced months of uncertainty and insecurity into Ted and his daughter's lives. This happened in March 2020. In October he was still regularly on the phone to Universal Credit seeking clarity about his benefit payments and repayments. In addition to his £1,000 debt for the advance payment, paid back at a rate of £80 a month, Ted also had prior deductions from his Tax Credits – the result of previous overpayments. Before the transfer to Universal Credit he had been repaying these at a rate of £1 per month – a negotiated rate because of his low income. Now, on Universal Credit, these were deducted at a rate of £39 per month. When his older daughter returned home from university, waiting to start a new job, the amount Ted could claim for their rent also reduced. Under increasing pressure, he contacted the DWP to see if he could reduce his repayments:

> So I sent a message ('Is there any way the reductions can be reduced? My energy bills are rising, already I can't make it through the month without [the] food bank. It's causing me to stress. Please can this be looked at?'). Reply: 'Unfortunately the repayment

amount of any advances you have had can't be changed as you agreed you could afford the amount when you took the advance. As you are also having other deductions taken you can call 0800 916 0647 to find out more about your debt repayments and ask if they can be reduced.' So I have rang them and their reply was I would have to prove hardship. I asked, how am I supposed to do that? She could not advise on how to do this. I said, would my bank statement do as it will show I'm already borrowing by the 14th of every month? She could not answer on how to prove hardship???????

Ted's story is one example of how seeking support from the social security system sometimes only further complicates an already difficult situation. In Ted's case a number of factors combined to leave him feeling 'stressed to the max' and insecure. Bureaucratic processes and their consequences were poorly communicated – in this case, that reporting a change of circumstances would trigger the transfer to Universal Credit. Furthermore, the design of the current system, with its five-week wait, advance payments and high level of repayments, pushed Ted into an unmanageable situation. For the first time ever, he needed to visit a food bank.

Ted's story is not unusual. Social security claims are often triggered by a crisis and a change of circumstances: losing a job, the breakdown of a relationship, moving house, the death of a loved one. At these times what people need is support, security and empathy. Instead, what they often get is complexity, bureaucracy and an inadequate level of cash support. To the poverty and hardship, the system adds degradation and humiliation, as Charlotte describes:

Life is always going to be slightly stressful during Covid but more so when you are on Universal Credit or a low income even whilst you are working. Personally for me I am on Universal Credit. I am finding this extremely difficult to live on. A lot of years ago I struggled to get a fridge freezer and only now as of next week I will finally get one. However

I have no working cooker at present and I am concerned about that heading towards Christmas. I do have a microwave so it's not too bad. I did try 3 times to apply for a non-repayable grant which is available but very hard to access and I was denied. It's awful as I am genuine and it's [an] appliance I need. When I phoned all those times I was demeaned and demoralised. I didn't feel like a human. I didn't feel respected as I felt like a rat. It's a horrible feeling.

During the pandemic, many people will have encountered the social security system for the first time. At the beginning of the first national lockdown ten times the usual number of new Universal Credit claims were made – 550,000 a week, compared to an average of 54,000 a week in the year before lockdown. Between 13 March and 14 May 2020 a total of 2.4 million new claims for Universal Credit were commenced.[16] To manage this sudden increase, the DWP introduced measures to make it easier to claim, suspending face-to-face appointments. They also redeployed staff from other areas to help process the influx. These measures were largely successful, and in this respect the department managed the crisis well. Even so, lots of people delayed making a claim because of uncertainty about whether they could. And once they did make a claim, they often found the process complicated and confusing,[17] and the support inadequate to their needs.

On the periphery

Policy-making during the pandemic continued to be influenced by concerns about so-called 'welfare dependency' and the need to encourage 'personal responsibility', narrowly construed as engagement in paid work. The influence of this was perhaps most obvious on one group in particular – those whose benefits were capped.

The benefit cap (see Chapter 1) was originally introduced, and is defended today, on the grounds of fairness. It places a limit on the total amount of benefits you can get, regardless of your circumstances. First announced by the then Chancellor

George Osborne at the 2010 Conservative Party conference, the cap came into effect in 2013, and was initially set at £26,000 per year – or £500 a week, the average family income at the time. Introducing the policy, Osborne declared, "No more open-ended cheque book. A maximum limit on benefits for those out of work. Set at the level the average working family earn … That is what the British people mean by fair."[18] The cap was subsequently reduced in 2016, and as of 2022 stands at £20,000 per year or £384.62 per week outside London, and £23,000 per year or £442.31 per week inside Greater London.

The policy was found to be popular, and recent accounts suggest that it was primarily introduced because it 'polled off the charts'.[19] The cap remained in place throughout the pandemic, meaning that those affected did not receive the £20 increase to Universal Credit. Aurora explained:

> We are capped on UC. I'm a widowed parent of two primary aged children. Our rent is over 95% of our total benefits. I have not been able to find work that fits around the children's school times. On top of it all, this month the government have taken money to pay for previous benefit overpayments (made when my late husband was dying). Our situation is precarious. We struggle enormously and have done for many reasons. I feel like an utter failure.

Central to the political argument for the benefit cap is the idea that families claiming financial support through social security should have to face the same choices and make the same 'calculations' as people who are working. This argument draws a distinction between 'responsible' individuals and families, who must make decisions based on their income, and 'irresponsible' people who are freed from difficult decisions and choices by the benefit system. Within this political narrative, Aurora's benefits had been capped to incentivise her to work, to take more responsibility for her choices, and to prevent her from becoming too 'dependent'.

This kind of thinking has underpinned many changes to social security since the 1980s. It is a way of thinking that sees the social security system as dangerous and addictive: as something that encourages dependency, that saps the capacity for responsibility and self-reliance, and that undermines the work ethic. As Aurora's difficult and painful situation makes clear, this kind of thinking is, at best, simple-minded and not grounded in evidence. As a basis for policy-making, it is responsible for innumerable harms and injustices, and has done enormous damage to people's lives. It has had particularly harsh consequences for those groups Aurora identifies – disabled people, carers and single parents – who, for different reasons, all find it difficult to support themselves (and their dependants) through the labour market alone.

Aurora did not make a 'decision' or a 'choice' to be bereaved. The high level of her benefits was also outside of her control. Aurora's benefits were capped, as in the vast majority of cases, because she lives in a metropolitan area with extremely high housing costs. The bulk of her 'benefit' money went to her (private) landlord. The cap effectively took away the money Aurora needed to run her household – to buy food, clothes for children, to pay bills. The rationale for subjecting her – and her children – to the difficult decisions this entailed was to encourage her to take 'personal responsibility' for herself by finding work. But this simplistic version of 'responsibility' – together with an equally one-dimensional view of 'dependency' – took little account of her other responsibilities as a parent, or of her children's dependency on her. It was experienced by Aurora as a form of punishment.

For Aurora, and others, the decision to exclude them from the £20 increase felt like an indication of how little their lives – and the lives of their children – mattered to society. At a time of extraordinary, unprecedented crisis, their needs were entirely ignored. As Aurora put it, '[f]rom what I can see, we are a group who will be swept under the carpet ... We already live on the periphery. How we will survive, I don't know.' This experience of being on the periphery, of being deemed unworthy of support is itself tied to processes of stigma and shame, which are too often, sadly, the bedfellows of poverty and social security receipt. Victoria was someone who did receive the £20 increase, but nonetheless she also described social security receipt as akin to punishment:

> While I've managed our budget well enough since I left my ex, my kids don't skip meals but I often do, and it hurts as mothers to be punished for something we have no control or choice over. I have literally nightmares most days over either our ex finding and killing us, or the government stopping my money and kids going hungry. All while trying to deal with a lifetime of ptsd in a culture where a single mum who's trying to access assistance for anything from food to childcare to mental health support is doubly criticised and punished. 'Why even have children if you can't provide for them?' Why make it so hard for single mothers to provide for their children? Why make women choose between physical safety and poverty? Why punish children and loving parents for the actions and inactions of abusive and absent parents? Stop blaming single mothers for not matching up to the systems designed to keep us down.

In the economic and social security response to the pandemic it is possible to see a clear hierarchy of concern. This hierarchy is not new, but reflects long-standing distinctions between people seen as 'deserving' and 'undeserving'. At the top of the hierarchy are those businesses and individuals who, because of their social position, were offered opportunities to profit and flourish. At the bottom, it seems, are families like Aurora's, denied even the temporary pandemic support because they are not in paid employment. Responding to the question 'How is your trust in government and the media?', Aurora wrote:

> The government has of course prioritised the economy. It is in their best interest to do so. As a family that lives well below the poverty line, we have borne the brunt of a system that has only punished the vulnerable. The majority being disabled, carers and/or single parent families. It has also been

perpetuated by most of the media. We are a rich country, where public money has been syphoned into private hands. Social security is becoming slowly eroded. We have been given scraps in order to placate us and the wider society.

Aurora outlines in very stark terms the different outcomes of the pandemic, according to social position. Looking around her, Aurora saw that those with the right connections and advantages were given opportunities for further enrichment, while people like herself were subjected to even greater hardship than before. She saw this not as accidental hardship, either, but as something intentionally inflicted on specific groups of people. The harm caused by the benefit cap is tied both to the financial support it denies Aurora and her family, but also to the wider messages it sends about the state's unwillingness to support her and families like hers.

'I've never felt so humiliated'

The stigma associated with benefits receipt pre-COVID-19 has been widely documented by researchers, charities and those experiencing it first-hand.[20] This chapter has already mentioned how, in the first two weeks of the first lockdown of 2020, there were more than ten times the usual number of Universal Credit claims. It would seem reasonable to imagine that such a sudden increase in people accessing social security benefits might have led to a change in perceptions. However, the increasing normality of benefits receipt amid the continued economic fallout of COVID-19 appeared to do little to alleviate the stigma associated with claiming social security. This suggests signs of the 'COVID exceptionalism' discussed earlier in the chapter, which was also evident in justifications for the policy-making response.[21] A survey of welfare attitudes in June 2021 found that 50.6% of Britons thought COVID-19 claimants were more likely to be deserving of support than pre-pandemic claimants, compared to only a quarter who thought they were likely to be equally deserving. New 'pandemic claimants' were perhaps identified as the unfortunate victims of a situation beyond their control. Fitting in with previous well-rehearsed tropes around deservingness and the social security system, pre-COVID claimants were much more likely to be seen as 'scroungers' – a judgement our families recognised all too well, as Charlotte shows:

> There is a stereotype about people on benefits being lazy and relying on the government too much. Recently in the media I was shocked to hear that some want Free School Meals abolished. Perhaps those people need to walk a mile in our shoes before making statements like that.

Diary entries regularly reflected on the stigma people experienced due to their poverty and benefits receipt. Jasmine, a survivor of domestic violence, set out the shame she felt in not being able to provide materially for her daughter:

> I decided to put my situation in words. I am 33 yrs old. My daughter is 13 yrs old. I am a single mum who escaped domestic violence from my own family a few years ago. I raise my daughter alone. I can honestly say the guilt I feel inside is something I can't explain. I can't afford internet so my child has not done homework. She has basically been that bored my child has become self destruct[ive].

For Rosie, this played out in different ways. She felt judged by someone she had thought a 'friend' when she found money to buy her children a treat:

> Bought the kids a well deserved treat after selling some old games on eBay. Told a 'friend' who commented 'thought you were skint?' Didn't realise I had to justify every penny I spend just because we don't have much. So much judgement of others around at the moment and it makes me so sad.

For Nellie, her experiences of stigma and shame were rooted in the very support that was meant to help her. She had repeated problems using her 'Healthy Start' vouchers. These means-tested vouchers are provided to pregnant women and parents of young children to help families access healthy food and milk. As Nellie explained:

> The bloody Healthy Start vouchers are haunting me again. If it wasn't already humiliating enough and down right inconvenient that I have to go to the shop in person to use them. Then I had the whole 'can't use 4 vouchers at once' debacle, for some inexplicable reason seemingly only to make things more difficult. This week's experience topped it all off. I've never felt so humiliated. Because I usually shop online (because it's the safer option during Covid and I spend less) I save my vouchers to use in a single shop once a month. All I buy are items covered by the vouchers. First humiliation – you can't use self-service, an actual person has to approve the voucher use. Second humiliation – because of Covid the supermarket has converted most of their checkouts to self service, there are only one or two manned checkouts, so I have a growing queue of people behind me. Because of the no more than 3 vouchers rule I have to split my shop and 'pay' twice, slowing the queue down even more.

In another diary entry, Nellie set out how this process of using her Healthy Start vouchers left her feeling completely humiliated. She concluded her diary entry with:

> The Healthy Start vouchers are just one small example of how the system stereotypes and discriminate[s] against people on low incomes/ benefits. The baseline assumption is one of mistrust. That this group of people will try and defraud the system. So they can't possibly be trusted to use the vouchers online, or at a self service checkout. And these people are so stupid that we have to make sure they use all the voucher money we're giving them

on healthy food because obviously all their own food choices are shit. Because £12.40 a month comes close to feeding a family of 4, 5 portions of fruit [and] veg a day! I'm done with it. I deserve to be trusted. To not feel humiliated. I can make healthy decisions for my family, I have a postgraduate qualification, my husband is a graduate. The school may get a pupil premium for my daughter but she is most certainly not an example of the attainment gap. I'm fed up of the assumption that people on benefits are untrustworthy and uneducated.

What Jasmine, Rosie and Nellie's accounts make clear is that people experiencing poverty are battling not only the material impact of hardship, but also the ways it affects how people see them, and how they see themselves. All too often, the social security system adds to, rather than reduces, the experience of stigma.

'I keep thinking I'm about to be punished for something'

Talk of a safety net implies something dependable. If you are falling, you want to be certain that the net will be there to stop you hitting the ground. But, as we saw in the preceding sections, rather than something that can be trusted to provide support when needed, participants often felt that the social security system was designed to punish them.

Over the course of two or three decades, entitlement to benefits has become increasingly conditional. This means that in order to qualify you must actively participate in 'work-related' activities (like CV-writing workshops), cooperate with work coaches and submit to various forms of monitoring and surveillance. This is true not only for job seekers – people deemed fit and able to work – but also for people claiming benefits on the grounds of disability and ill health, who are required to demonstrate how they are 'preparing' for a return to work. If people fail to comply – or are judged as not cooperating – then they receive a sanction. That is, their benefits stop. With Universal Credit, this system now also extends to people in work, who are required to demonstrate what they are doing to find more hours or a better-paid job.

The expansion of conditionality has led to the proliferation of bureaucratic systems and processes for monitoring, testing and checking up on claimants. This is often described by politicians and policy makers as 'support', but in reality there is often little on offer that people find appropriate or useful. For example, here is Connie describing her experience of the support available:

> I claim Universal Credit and hate how the system makes me feel for that. I don't work enough hours for them, so they frequently send links to job fairs or job roles, despite them having no idea of my skill set and abilities. I was recently sent a link for construction jobs, bearing in mind that my working life has been mainly in the public and voluntary sectors, I'm not sure how they thought I might be qualified to start building houses.

Rather than supported, the system of conditionality leaves people feeling demeaned and demoralised, and has contributed to a widespread atmosphere of worry and suspicion.[22]

Alongside the other measures announced in March 2020, much of the system for monitoring what claimants were doing to find work was also suspended. From March until July 2020, face-to-face appointments stopped. The general requirement to be searching for work, and specific requirements about time spent searching for work and the number of jobs to apply for, were all temporarily suspended. This lasted for the duration of the first lockdown. Having intentionally pulled the stop cord on the economy, it was not reasonable for the government to require that people look for work. Yet, during this period, people continued to search for work,[23] undermining yet further the logic for conditionality and compulsion. As the country slowly emerged from lockdown, and despite calls for them to be suspended for the duration of pandemic, conditionality and sanctions were reintroduced in July 2020.

This was a cause for concern for many claimants. Here is Victoria:

Well, I'm now having a mild panic attack. Message on my universal credit account today telling me someone is ringing me tomorrow to review my account. I'm not sure if it's a normal part of the job centres reopening or if I've done something wrong (it's written in a rather cold and direct way, with more emphasis on the dangers of not taking the call, such as sanctions, than what the call is about), so I'm panicking about it and can't mentally prepare myself for a phone call that I don't know why or what it's about and I keep thinking I'm about to be punished for something.

Victoria's fears were understandable. Indeed, figures from the DWP show levels of benefit sanctions rising to above pre-pandemic rates, with almost 50,000 people on Universal Credit sanctioned in November 2021, significantly more than the pre-pandemic peak of 36,780 in October 2019.[24] While this is less than 1% of all claimants, the threat and the consequent fear of sanctions is ever-present, potentially affecting all claimants subject to conditionality, and gives all interactions with the DWP and the Jobcentre a firm punitive edge. This comes across especially strongly in a series of entries by Charlotte, a former teacher and single mother of two school-age children. Charlotte's eldest started secondary school in September 2020, and it had been Charlotte's intention to make this a moment of transition for the whole family and look to start work again around that time. These plans were derailed by the pandemic. Instead, Charlotte found herself home schooling her children, while also being required to meet the work search conditions of her benefit claim. In the summer of 2020 she wrote:

I was shocked to receive a phone call from Medical Assessors from Universal Credit on Friday 17th July. The man who called me was very curt and very aggressive in his demeanour. He basically threatened that my money was going to be stopped if I didn't show signs of getting a job. I asked him quite nicely about what the government were implementing to help single parents to home school but also look for jobs and child care etc. He basically told me he was the messenger and that another call would come next week and then they would make decisions about my universal credit. I'm terrified.

The next day, Charlotte returned to her diary to record another entry:

The Universal credit system is flawed. I am currently being forced to look for work and to show evidence of looking 'online' for work for over 20 hours a week. With no wifi and having to pay for data I am unsure of how that is physically possible. I am also expected to homeschool my 6 year old 3 days every week and my daughter 2 weeks in every month. I cannot see how a job will work. The pressure is immense and there's the threat of UC stopping payments.

Conditionality and sanctions have been justified in various ways, with ideas that are often poorly evidenced. Not only that, but also the emphasis on paid work, whatever the circumstances, devalues the labour of care and parenting – it fails to recognise unpaid work – while making it harder (for some people) to choose to prioritise this work. When the government temporarily suspended conditionality and sanctions, research evidence[25] showed that people still looked for work, even at a time of lockdown and when job vacancies were hard to find. This raises the questions: why not replace conditionality with meaningful, person-centred support? Despite decades of rhetorical bluster about the extensive support on offer to social security claimants (often used to justify increasingly punitive measures), it is something that participants in Covid Realities returned to again and again as entirely lacking, but urgently needed.

Making social security work for us all

This chapter began with Rishi Sunak setting out a raft of unprecedented measures to temporarily repair and strengthen the safety net. It outlined some of the ways that these measures, although welcome, were nonetheless inadequate to people's needs. The policy failure we have highlighted here is three-fold. First, there was a failure to act effectively in providing adequate support to families in poverty. Second, there was a failure to provide security to families, who were instead left in an anxious state of limbo as they awaited news about whether and when temporary measures would end. Third, there has been a failure of imagination; to step outside and beyond tired, divisive narratives of 'workers' and 'welfare dependents', and instead to acknowledge what the pandemic has demonstrated again and again, and in various ways: that our common humanity is to be found in our dependencies on one another.

It is for this reason that thinking in terms of a 'safety net' isn't always the best analogy for thinking about social security support. This analogy sees us as most fully human when we are independent and alone, crossing the void with only the barest minimum of support. One thing that Covid Realities has emphasised is that this is a very poor conception of what it means to be a person. The vision of freedom implicit in many of these pages is one defined less by independence from others than by the ability to actively support others and shape our relationships with them. It is about our capacity to act from within the inescapable dependencies that necessarily define us. Dependencies which should be celebrated rather than condemned.

In this chapter, and across this book, as we have shared the accounts of families living in poverty through COVID-19, our writing has often been fuelled by anger. Anger that we live in a society where it is deemed okay for people to routinely go without. Anger that it has become commonplace to assume that individual failings are to blame for poverty, rather than economic structures and social relationships. And anger that even during this crisis, it has too often felt like families on a low income were forgotten rather than targeted for help and support. It is easy (and understandable) to direct much of this anger at Boris Johnson's Conservative government and their many failures.

Scrutinising the action – or inaction – of our political leaders during COVID-19 is essential, and will be a key focus of the promised independent inquiry, but we also need to adopt a wider lens, taking in the leaders who had left Britain so ill-equipped to weather the incoming storm. Here, David Cameron and George Osborne need to be placed under the spotlight. The decade of austerity that they oversaw shrivelled and weakened the welfare state, and left our public services ill-equipped to cope at any time, let alone during the extraordinary circumstances of a global pandemic. While the groundwork of 'austerity' was firmly laid by Cameron and Osborne's predecessors, the Conservative-led coalition's austerity project was distinct from what came before: the rhetoric was harsher and the cuts were deeper and more punitive. Cameron and Osborne may not have been our political leaders during this crisis, but they engineered the boat in which we sailed into the storm: a leaky, beleaguered vessel.

The everyday realities shared across this book have starkly illustrated the harms that repeated cuts to social security have wrought, harms that we must always remember are chosen, and not inevitable. In the next, concluding chapter, we set out a different way forward, exploring what is needed to re-embed social security as a vital part of our nation's social fabric.

Rather than view the social security system as something that diminishes and demoralises us, that erodes a sacrosanct ethic of work, we should instead acknowledge the things it might make possible – the care, learning, health, skills, talents and relationships that it can support and nurture. Social security, properly conceptualised and delivered, can be a force for good, and one of universal value. We need to work together to build a social security system that works with, rather than against, the grain of everyday lives and the realities of all of our dependencies on each other. Read on to find out how we might begin that task.

Conclusion
Our manifesto for change

Led by Ruth and Maddy

It's hard to write about the past when the present feels so suffocating. Before covid feels like a lifetime ago. So much has changed since then.

Victoria

Government hands should hold us — they should catch us.

Rosie

In the time since the pandemic began, I have changed, we have all changed. Whilst I had hoped for a different world, after the silence and stillness of lockdown, I knew it was a big hope.

I had hoped we would take comfort from one another and want to emerge better.

I will not be silent
Because it suits you
I will not starve because
You do not care

Poverty is not simply about no food or heating. It creates a lack of resilience, a lack of spontaneity that our kids thrive upon, that serves them well in decision making going forward. We need to change the narrative to become better. Let's hope that happens. It's our story.

Lois

Hoping for a better future: our manifesto for change

This book is not, and could never be, an easy read. Charting the first year of the pandemic for families living on a low income provides unforgiving insight into the inadequacies of our social security system, detailing the many ways in which what is regularly described as a safety net is all too often anything but. In the preceding chapters, we heard from parents about the difficult choices they face when money is running out, and about how the careful balance of getting by in poverty was suddenly made impossible when COVID-19 hit. We heard about the inevitable impact this had on children – children who were already facing the disruption of school closures, the isolation of repeated lockdowns and restrictions on everyday contact. We also heard how the worry and insecurity caused by poverty damages parents' mental health, placing families under greater strain.

What we have seen is that parents and carers facing poverty during the pandemic endured multiple insecurities: the uncertainty of living through and having to cope with COVID-19 was compounded by the very specific insecurities that poverty and insufficient income create. These insecurities intersect and connect in difficult and distressing ways. The return to school after a lockdown, for example, creates worry about how your child will cope, but also anxiety about how you will afford the new school uniform they need after a growth spurt. We have also seen the ways that parents navigated this new terrain, doing all they could to protect their children from hardship, budgeting carefully and trying to create normality during anything but normal times. We have seen parents experiencing stigma because of being in receipt of benefits, a stigma that often prevents them from accessing the support that they need.

There are things, however, that we have not seen, that have been absent. Sadly, we have not seen state action to provide the support that is so urgently needed. We have not seen the government dedicate targeted support to families with children through the social security system at any point during the pandemic, despite the very clear evidence of unmet and pressing need. Neither have we seen the government make a case for keeping the £20 increase to Universal Credit, as part of an investment in both social security and those who need it at some point in their lives. And we have not seen the government show a proper understanding of the everyday realities of life on a low income, or a willingness to listen and learn about these realities, in order to act on them and try to make things better. Those of us familiar with the history of poverty and inequality in the UK should probably not be surprised by any of this.

But it is inexcusable all the same that, in a time of unprecedented crisis, so little was done to support families experiencing poverty, with the £20 increase to Universal Credit always only a temporary and partial fix. This temporary increase, and the surrounding debate, is itself symbolic of much that is wrong not only with this government's approach to social security, but also with our broader attitude towards social security as a society. On the one hand, the increase was a recognition, in a moment of crisis, that some people's needs were not being met; on the other hand, this was a minimal form of recognition that seemed carefully calibrated to close down much-needed conversations. It avoided crucial discussions about the longer-term reasons why the increase was necessary, and signalled a refusal to face up to the true depth and extent of poverty and hardship in contemporary Britain. It also avoided a long-overdue engagement with the fact that 'dependency', far from being something shameful, is a universal truth at the heart of everyone's lives.

In this concluding chapter, we set out how things could be different: a manifesto for change. This manifesto is rooted in just four words: expertise, hope, care and change. We think each of these words is vital if we are to see a better post-pandemic world. This manifesto has been developed in partnership with the parents and carers living on a low income who together make up Covid Realities.

Expertise

If we are to change our country's social security system, we need to radically change whom we think of as the experts, and how we involve people with experiences of poverty in the policy-making processes that will directly affect them. When Universal Credit was first rolled out, DWP officials celebrated their 'test and learn' approach: testing the new benefit on a small number of claimants and then learning lessons before making any amendments needed. A willingness to 'test' social security policies on people (and people who are at a point of need), rather than actually listening and engaging with those same people first, is itself indicative of much that is wrong with current policy-making.

Indeed, it is hard to overstate how much more can and should be done to engage with and learn from the expertise that comes from, and can only come from, everyday lived experiences of the area in which policy is being developed. We all lose out if we do not include this form of expertise in our policy-making. Returning to Universal Credit, had the government adopted a 'listen and learn' approach, rather than 'test and learn', it would have identified, at an early stage, design flaws with the benefit and helped to prevent unnecessary hardship caused by misguided policy decisions. People with the expertise born of experience would have identified problems with a once-monthly payment, with housing payments going directly to claimants, and with a shift to in-work conditionality. These design features could have been changed, and experts by experience could have contributed towards making the benefit better for everyone.

Significantly, though, the involvement and participation of experts by experience – in policy making and in the wider debate surrounding it facilitated by the media, think-tanks and academics – is not only about bringing new expertise to the table. It is also about challenging the broader misrecognition that people experiencing poverty face when they are talked about, problematised, stereotyped, caricatured, but so seldom actually heard. We saw earlier how poverty is a site of injustice. Properly valuing lived experiences of poverty can make a contribution to countering the misrecognition and disrespect people in poverty routinely encounter.

People with direct experiences of poverty and social security are a central part of much-needed efforts to challenge the 'machine of anti-welfare commonsense' that we discussed earlier in the book, which steamrolls through policy making in an incredibly damaging way. This anti-welfare commonsense, which pits worker against workless and implies that poverty is a result of poor choices, poor behaviour and poor morals, allowed politicians to decimate our social security system under the Conservative-led coalition government. And it allowed Boris Johnson's government licence to act decisively on furlough and job retention (within a framing of help for deserving workers), and yet to do almost nothing for families experiencing poverty and hardship. Working in imaginative and creative ways, people with direct experiences of poverty and social security can challenge this dominant narrative. We already see this in work done by anti-poverty groups like Poverty2Solutions and the APLE Collective, and also in the actions taken by Covid Realities participants themselves. From creating a zine, to documenting life on a low income through COVID, to writing sections of this book and recording audio for short videos capturing lived experiences, participants have contributed alternative, radical narratives that show their labour, agency and – perhaps above all – hope.

Hope

It is hard to respond calmly to the government's policy choices during the pandemic, especially given that they have been justified in a way that sometimes suggests policy-making in ignorance or even in spite of the evidence base. In Autumn 2021, as the government tried to defend pressing ahead with the £20 cut to Universal Credit, Boris Johnson repeatedly seemed to draw a distinction between supporting work and welfare: obscuring the fact that over a third of Universal Credit claimants are already in work. Work and Pensions Secretary Thérèse Coffey also encouraged claimants to work an additional two hours a week to offset the loss, ignoring the reality that people would have to work an extra *nine* hours to make up the cut. Having hope when are politicians are quite this ill-informed is not easy.

However hard, we do need to find places for hope and reasons to be hopeful. Our starting point for hopefulness must be the pandemic itself, and the ways in which moments of crisis are also moments of rupture that bring with them the possibilities of change. We all know the story of how the circumstances of the Second World War led to the birth of the welfare state, and while the present account neglects much that was wrong with our 'golden age of welfare', it is a reminder that crises can be a trigger for radical reform. But the changes that come are not always positive ones. We saw this in the aftermath of the global financial crisis of 2008–09, which led to a resurgence of neoliberalism and rising authoritarianism and nationalism across much of the world. With the pandemic, early talk of the need to 'build back better' seems to have been replaced by the everyday work of living through the latter (and increasingly unpredictable) stages of the pandemic and all of our efforts to find a way to navigate the 'new normal'.

But these calls to 'build back better' need to be mobilised. There are key learnings from the pandemic that we can take with us as we try and set out possibilities for a different and better future, learnings that should help us to identify and pursue opportunities for change.

First, and most important of all, perhaps, is the hope we can take from many everyday responses to the pandemic. As writer, historian and activist Rebecca Solnit reminds us,[1] disaster responses often assume that, in times of national (or global) disaster, the worst aspects of human nature will emerge. In fact, and as we witnessed in the pandemic, people are typically resourceful, altruistic and creative. We saw this in the UK, and elsewhere, with the emergence of mutual aid groups, a response from people looking to care for and support one another at a time of crisis. This caring and altruistic response to disasters, which Solnit charts, was also evident in people's willingness to withdraw from shared spaces to protect one another – by social distancing and self-isolating – an act of withdrawal that Solnit describes as an act of solidarity.

The pandemic demonstrated the possibilities of state intervention, and on a massive scale. When Rishi Sunak set out (as he did on several occasions) his pandemic rescue package, he also threw away the old certainties, often drawn along political party lines, of where and when the state can intervene. Furlough showed that the British state can provide earning-replacement schemes – it can pay people's wages – when the public and political will is there. The (albeit temporary) suspension of welfare conditionality at the height of the pandemic underscored the possibility of a social security system without punitive work requirements as its cornerstone. What the possibilities of state intervention show us is that a failure to act is always a political choice, and we can all do more to make sure politicians are accountable both for what they do and for what they fail to do.

A further learning from the pandemic consists of the acts of unity and resistance – of solidarity – that can be created even at a time of immense strain. In Covid Realities, parents and carers from across the UK joined together, sharing experiences over Zoom, offering support to each other and finding imaginative and creative ways to share their accounts with politicians and – through media appearances – sometimes with millions of people. Importantly, too, the new ways of working that the pandemic forced us to adopt created exciting and novel possibilities. We shifted to working online, virtually connecting parents and creating a national conversation about poverty and, critically, about change. There is a power in solidarity, especially for those who experience poverty and the stigma and shame so often associated with it.

The final learning that we must take from the pandemic, but also from the accounts shared in this book, is of the urgent need to act. The social security system entered the pandemic in poor health, and without reform we will see child poverty soar. In 2021 alone, child poverty will have cost the UK £38 billion,[2] and there is no figure that can be placed on the human cost of poverty. Britain needs a social security system that offers dignity and respect to all those who use it, and that is seen as a core part of our social settlement. The time to build that social security system is now.

In a 2016 essay,[3] Rebecca Solnit sets out how hope is an embrace of the unknown, more productive than optimism and pessimism because it creates a space where what each of us does (or, indeed, does not do) can make a difference. She says: 'hope locates itself in the premises that we don't know what will happen and in the spaciousness of uncertainty is room to act'. As we hope for a post-pandemic future, we all face uncertainty and fears about what might come next. But we all need to hold on to and act with hope.

EXPERIENCE tomorrow WITH LOVE

time... for COMMUNITY

Inspiring Our communities

one future

CHANGE OUR STORY

Supporting EVERYONE

Kim 2021

Care

Changing perceptions of social security is a difficult task. But it will be made easier if we all try to move our focus away from 'work' and instead towards 'care'. When we speak of 'care', here we are using the term in its broadest sense, like the Care Collective,[4] a London-based group of researchers and activists aiming to understand and address the multiple and extreme crises of care. We mean the unpaid care that happens in families, and the practical, paid care that workers do in care homes, schools and hospitals. But we also mean the care of activists campaigning for policies that reduce fossil fuel use, the care of Covid Realities participants in coming together to support each other and call for change, and the care built into policies that improve people's lives and protect the environment. So care is an individual activity, in which we reach out to and support others, but it is also a political and collective act, to improve the conditions of society for all of us. We need to reassess what we need and what we value in society, and we need to recognise the fundamental importance of care – both paid and unpaid.

The pandemic exposed how much we all rely on carers and how badly our current economic system and societal structures support this work. It also exposed how the work of parenting needs to be better recognised and valued. This means enabling people to choose and prioritise this work above paid work in the labour market, and to receive financial support to do so. It also means widespread access to affordable, high-quality childcare. The pandemic revealed what happens when our societal structures simply fail to care, instead performing what Doreen Lawrence characterises as 'institutional indifference'[5] towards those experiencing poverty, disability, discrimination and other (often overlapping) vulnerabilities. This failure to care predates the pandemic and meant that we entered it almost spectacularly ill-equipped to get through it.[6]

At the height of the crisis as we all clapped for carers it felt like change might just come, as if there might be a rebalancing towards embracing and rewarding care. But that change now seems less likely, set against a context where both main parties are once again competing to be seen as the party of 'working people'. Pledges to support 'hardworking families' and 'working people' are used by politicians to signal who they judge to be deserving of state support, with only silence where support for those unable to work should be. Despite the pandemic rhetoric, we sadly have both main political parties refusing to stand up and advocate for care, and for action to support those carrying out unpaid but hugely vital care work.

What the pandemic also exposed is that we all want to have time to care. But all too often the way our labour market is set up fails to recognise this. It is still too difficult for parents to work flexibly, or to have proper paid time off when their children are young or in need.

As a society, as individuals, and as change makers, we need to allow ourselves to give more space and time for care; for the doing of it, and for the working towards change that allows it to be possible, and for it to be better recognised in our labour market. We need to recognise the gendered, racialised, classed and overlapping disadvantages that arise from our reliance on low-paid, insecure care workers who do such vital work caring for children, for disabled people and for older people. And we need to recognise that there is still much, much more to do to get us away from a blinkered focus on getting people into paid work – and any work – rather than creating systems that allow us to make a positive choice to prioritise care.

Change

Prioritising care is a starting point for change, bringing with it the prospect of rethinking broader debates around social security, poverty and inequality in ways that can help to lay the groundwork for better, more sustainable systems of support. To make change happen, you first need a vision of what the future should look like. Through Covid Realities, participants developed their vision for a different social security system, and a core set of principles (see Figure 2). This is their agenda for change.

Our collective vision is for a social security system that is understanding and compassionate, treats people with dignity and respect, and offers meaningful opportunities and support.

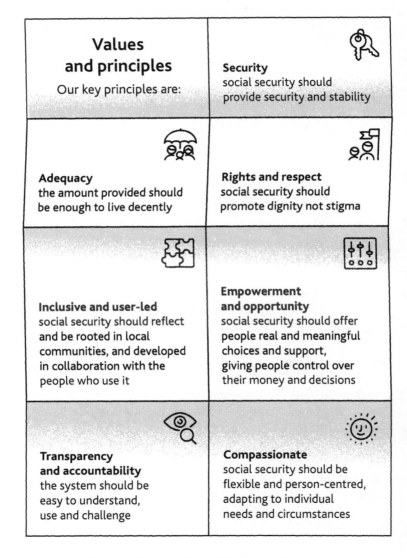

Values and principles Our key principles are:	Security social security should provide security and stability
Adequacy the amount provided should be enough to live decently	**Rights and respect** social security should promote dignity not stigma
Inclusive and user-led social security should reflect and be rooted in local communities, and developed in collaboration with the people who use it	**Empowerment and opportunity** social security should offer people real and meaningful choices and support, giving people control over their money and decisions
Transparency and accountability the system should be easy to understand, use and challenge	**Compassionate** social security should be flexible and person-centred, adapting to individual needs and circumstances

Figure 2: Visions and principles for a better future

This vision and the related principles are marked in both their breadth and ambition. But what is perhaps most remarkable of all is the fact that what parents and carers are calling for seems perfectly reasonable (and arguably modest), yet feels simultaneously difficult to achieve. Such is the gulf between what they are calling for and the ways in which our social security system in the UK currently operates.

In a series of 'Big Ideas' groups (online discussion sessions, held by Zoom), participants in Covid Realities worked together to flesh out and develop recommendations for policy changes that would begin to realise their vision. These were focused around changes to social security support for families with children; improvements in the relationship between claimants and the DWP; and suggestions for how policy makers and the wider research community could better work with and involve the expertise that comes with experiences of social security and poverty. Changes that participants sought included improvements to the adequacy of social security (increasing child benefit for each and every child by £10 a week, reversing the £20 cut to Universal Credit and extending it to legacy benefit claimants, for example), as well as lower-cost but no less transformational changes (such as improving the transparency in communications with DWP, and having a right to be treated with dignity and respect). Work by Child Poverty Action Group to model the collective impact of the changes showed that the package had the scope to lift 1.4 million children out of poverty. Changes well worth making, then.

These changes are focused both on the need for increased financial support for families in poverty and also on the need for better recognition and respect for those experiencing poverty in the UK.

Our reformist lens focuses on the social security system, while recognising that there is a need for much broader, fundamental change, looking at the paid labour market and the wider reliance on neoliberalism and what some call 'robber-baron capitalism'. With the climate crisis bound to dwarf the pandemic in its reach and impact, there is urgent work needed to better understand the place for an improved social security system within any Green New Deal. Here, a focus on sustainability is helpful, reminding us all of the need to find ways to create sustainable lives, sustainable societies and, ultimately, a sustainable world.

Looking specifically at social security, though, there are key things to keep in mind when trying to build a better future.

Poverty is fundamentally about ...

Politicians, policy makers, commentators and all of us need to be honest about what drives poverty, and what might solve it. Money. Or, rather, its absence. Poverty is fundamentally about a lack of material resources, and it can only be properly addressed by cash (and it should be cash) transfers. The explosion of food banks across the UK – and also of 'baby banks', 'beauty banks', 'school uniform banks' – has occurred as a direct result of austerity. But what has also happened is that we have witnessed a broader fragmentation of poverty,[7] with people talking not of a problem of poverty, but of a problem of 'food poverty', of 'hygiene poverty', even of 'furniture poverty' or 'pet poverty'. These new terms risk obscuring the fact that all of these supposedly different types of poverty are about the absence of a sufficient income to afford the essentials to support oneself and one's family. There is a danger that a focus on these poverty 'types' also triggers a partial, paternalistic and, often, stigmatising response. When the problem of poverty is broken up and presented as 'food poverty' – a question of someone having inadequate food for themselves and their family – then the solution becomes to provide food, today largely in the form of charitable provision through food banks. These organisations provide predefined parcels of sometimes nutritionally inadequate and often culturally inappropriate food, itself obtained through the recycling of waste food or corporate-led supermarket initiatives. But these supposed solutions enable the state to step back, and deny people agency and choice. They all too often strip individuals of their dignity, requiring invasive referrals and questioning before people can receive the food-based support being offered.

While we would be the last people to want to criticise Marcus Rashford and his heroic campaigning efforts on poverty, there have been times when this campaign has seemed to be on the verge of falling into this 'fragmentation of poverty' trap. It is great to hear him speak about the 'child hunger pandemic', but it is worth stopping to think about why children are hungry, and, if children are hungry, isn't it likely that their parents are hungry too? A 'child hunger pandemic' is also an 'adult and family hunger pandemic', which is not caused by an absence of food but by an absence of money to purchase adequate food.

Addressing this is not easy, and requires us to ask hard questions about the root of 'food poverty' or 'period poverty' and to call for solutions that are effective in addressing this root, prioritising money rather than food or sanitary products. Children living in poverty are not best served by a new food bank opening up around the corner from them, or their parents being able to get a new-to-them bed from a 'furniture poverty' coalition of bed manufacturers and charities. They are best served by their parents having access to enough income so that they can make their own choices, and so it is calls to make sure that all families have enough income that we need to prioritise.

We must take an intersectional lens

Most of you who have read this far into the book will (we hope) be persuaded of the need to take action on poverty, and to repair and improve our threadbare social security system. But what we must also do, and what is not said enough, especially in a predominantly White (and still too male, able-bodied) social policy world, is that we all need to take an intersectional lens when we analyse poverty.

We need to look not just at how class *or* gender *or* ethnicity impact on lived experiences but how these, and other characteristics, overlap to shape how someone experiences the world, as well as the ways in which they are subject to discrimination or disadvantage, whether this is within institutions, by other individuals or by certain government policies.

The pandemic amplified the extent of these intersecting inequalities and their impact. Most devastatingly of all, the mortality risks of COVID-19 were related to someone's ethnicity, their income group and their employment type (and status) in ways that meant that White, rich, white-collar workers had the highest chance of surviving the pandemic. This was a consequence not of the behaviour or health consciousness of White, rich, white-collar workers but, rather, of the histories of advantage, and the current systems and policies maintaining that advantage. They were, for example, more likely than people from racially minoritised groups and people on low incomes to work in jobs where they could work at home, placing them at lower exposure to the virus.

Taking an intersectional lens is crucial to any discussion of poverty, as it helps us to identify the varying ways in which people are discriminated against. The absence of an intersectional lens in studies of poverty is partly a consequence of the lack of diversity among the research community itself. The Whiteness of the social policy research community itself reflects institutionalised racism and barriers that racially minoritised populations experience in accessing higher education and securing research grants and stable employment.[8] The relative lack of diversity among the research community (and barriers according to ethnicity, disability and gender) inevitably impacts research undertaken and relationships with Black, disabled and other marginalised populations.

We are keenly aware that this is a book about poverty written by an all-White team, which is itself a failing and is symptomatic of wider diversity problems within social policy. Ethnicity does not feature as a key theme in the book, despite the greater likelihood of racially minoritised groups to experience poverty, rather than the White majority. While we engaged with a range of participants in Covid Realities, we have not done as much as we could – and should – to explore the intersectionality of people's experiences, and our portrayal of the lived experiences of the COVID-19 pandemic is the poorer for it. These are failings that we must own and take forward, with the intention of focusing more on intersectionality in future work and collaborating with researchers and participants from minority communities to expand the scope and complexity of our research.

Moving out of the poverty silo: connecting with wider crises and drawing conceptual alliances

While we are on the subject of our own failings, it is important to also state frankly that this book (and the wider research) follows a long tradition in mainstream social policy of focusing very squarely on the 'problem of poverty'. It does not do enough to show how poverty can be seen as symptomatic of wider societal failings that demand us to shift our interrogatory lens upwards. As R.H. Tawney famously put it: 'What thoughtful rich people call the problem of poverty, thoughtful poor people with equal justice call the problem of riches.'

With Covid Realities, we have been motivated to work with parents and carers experiencing poverty to document their lives during a pandemic, drawing out the many ways in which they have so often been failed by the welfare state and wider societal structures. We can see a defensible logic in this, especially given our collaborative, participatory approach. All the same, there is inevitably a risk that this singular focus on life on a low income conceals the parallel need to understand how those living, for example, with great wealth experience times of crisis, or to pay attention to how social policies so often create experiences of social control for those in poverty, but only the occasional, well-intentioned (and often carrot-incentivised) nudge for those higher up the income spectrum. There is also a risk that we do not do (and in our work have not done) enough to draw out the connections between poverty and inequality, showing the many harms that inequality does to each and every one of us. Inequality can help here to build a unifying call for change. While poverty is a social harm that requires corrective action, inequality – as first Kate Pickett and Richard Wilkinson,[9] and then Thomas Piketty,[10] have so effectively demonstrated – harms us all, even if we do not experience the specific (and widespread) hardships associated with life on the lowest end of the income scale.

But even more boldly, and as argued by Fiona Williams,[11] we need to do more to connect central societal challenges (perhaps best understood as crises) with each other, drawing out and building alliances between – for example – those who challenge the crises of climate, austerity and care.

Converting calls for change into practical asks

Running through this chapter is a call for radical and imaginative change that would recast social security as a public good and as a central part of a social settlement fit for our post-pandemic times. Here, we are inspired by researcher and activist Ruth Levitas,[12] who calls for the adoption of utopia (and utopian thinking) as a method for thinking about and researching the world. Ruth Levitas encourages us to consider what *should* be (rather than only what feels possible). This creates space for us to think imaginatively about possible futures, thinking that can still be critical and reflective, but that is not constrained by current contexts.

As well as a need to embrace utopian thinking, we must also respond to the urgency of the situation, and make the case for immediate, practical changes that would make a significant difference to the lives of millions of households.

As campaigners will tell you, there are difficult choices to be made between demands that are ambitious (but perhaps unlikely to be realised) and ones that seem more feasible, but perhaps do not go far enough to properly address the challenges and crises we face. There are real trade-offs here, and ones that we discussed in our Big Ideas groups as we talked together about post-pandemic futures. What felt most helpful, for us, was to anchor all calls for change within broader principles of adequacy and security. This can be framed as part of a wider narrative of care: our systems need to show they care.

From this perspective, even relatively modest changes are part of broader ambitions for a social security system that grants security to claimants, offers respectful and dignified treatment and provides adequate support. A particular example here is the Universal Credit online journal, in which claimants are required to record job searches and may communicate with DWP staff (also known as work coaches) and vice versa. At the moment, claimants can write long messages in their journal, setting out fears about changes in payments, or asking questions about what might happen if their circumstances change. And then claimants wait. And wait. And all too often hear nothing back, or get an auto response advising them to look online. This process contrasts starkly with what happens if a work coach sends a message to a claimant asking for information or requesting that they undertake a specified work-related activity. Then the claimant must respond, and speedily, or risk benefit sanctions. This lopsided and profoundly unequal dynamic reinforces the relationship that exists between a claimant and their work coach, a relationship where all the power sits with the DWP. So, even though giving claimants a right of reply to their own journal messages might sound small fry, even tokenistic, it would make a significant break with current policy, and would signal intent to treat claimants with respect. And that's why it matters. It is these small, practical and substantive policy asks that underpin and are crucial stepping stones towards more radical change.

Hoping and acting together

At the start of this chapter we talked about the vital place for hope in trying to carve out a post-pandemic future. We emphasised the need to use hope as a spur to action, and for all of us to recognise the contribution we can make to carving out a future that is better than what has come before. As readers of this book, you are already – we hope – invested in the need to rebuild our social security system. This work needs to begin now. In November 2021, participants came together online to think about what action they would like readers of this book to take. On the following pages you will find a list from that meeting, things that each and every one of us can do to start the work to build a better future.

In that meeting, Lexie and Victoria B described how easy it is to simply feel powerless: as if it is impossible to do anything when the scale of the challenge is so big. But they wanted each of you to know that you do have power, that by taking just one of the actions suggested below you can be part of calling for change.

Doing these things may feel pointless in a political context in which the denigration and dismantling of 'welfare' seems to continue, despite all that the pandemic exposed. It is anything but. As Rebecca Solnit reminds us, for change to come, we all need to 'tell other stories about who we are, what we want and what is possible'. Covid Realities has been an effort to do just that. And it is an effort that can, with your help, continue and grow.

Making change together
You've read the book, now what?

It's been a year like no other, and we want change to address the challenges families have faced.

Covid Realities participants would like
to thank you for reading the book
and ask you to do as many
of the following as you can.

Figure 3: What can you do that is hopeful and will make change happen?

- [ ] If you are on a low income, know that you are not alone. Reach out for help and advice if you need it (for example, from Citizens Advice or mental health charities).

- [ ] Recognise that there are many reasons people need support from our social security system, and that there should be no shame in this.

- [ ] Get the message out there that many of us will depend on social security at some point in our lives. We all benefit from social security – there is no 'them' and 'us'.

- [ ] Do your own research to find out more about the benefits system – form your own opinions and don't be led by media representations.

- [ ] Be vocal about and challenge inequalities whenever you see them.

- [ ] Demand more of your politicians – lobby them for action on poverty.

- [ ] If you can, help create opportunities for people with experiences of poverty and social security to speak out, to share their experiences, and to set out what needs to change.

- [ ] Help us to shift society's views and to share human stories of the realities of life on a low income.

- [ ] Talk to family and friends about what you've read, and share it on social media and with wider networks.

- [ ] Pass this book on!

Cat, a participant in Covid Realities, spoke at a parliamentary event that took place in March 2021 to mark a year since the first national lockdown. Cat speaks for all of us when she set out the changes that are needed:

> 'We're asking for a fundamental change in the way we are seen and treated within the system.
>
> We want to be respected enough to not have to prove ourselves at every single turn.
>
> We want enough money to live on so we can concentrate on improving our lot.
>
> We want the common courtesy of advanced notice, clear explanations, appointments on time, and reciprocal understanding when things don't happen as planned.
>
> We want work coaches to actually support us, encourage us, and believe in us.
>
> We want to be met with dignity and respect, as equals.
>
> If society sees the government viewing us differently, support us properly, treating us well, caring about us, then slowly it will too.
>
> Remove the stereotypes and talk to us as equals.
>
> Not scroungers. Not layabouts. Not uneducated.
>
> But as human beings, just like you, trying to do the best for our families.
>
> Just like you.'

Afterword

This is no way for anyone to have to live

Led by Katie

This is no way for anyone to have to live in the twenty-first century.

Anon

The Autumn Budget brought some relief as we saw the taper rate reduced by only 8p. The rate before you start losing your income increased by £40 a month but this doesn't go far enough as we see a rise in living costs from all suppliers, in our food and services. However, there's still so many not thought of at all. Those on the benefit cap and legacy benefits still struggling through. Universal Credit is creating a circle of debt, it is creating a level of fear and insecurity that is making people ill. I have had to cancel hospital appointments earlier this year as I couldn't afford to isolate for 3 days with no income never mind travel 180 miles for a 5 min appointment, especially when I'm already having to make choices on heating my home or food on the table. My health has been impacted and I have had to have counselling to help me manage my pain.

Helen

I must admit – I didn't bother tuning in for the Spring statement, because that's how demoralised I feel right now. I couldn't face it. I was sure it would have nothing to offer folk like me in receipt of legacy benefits. How right I was – it offered exactly nothing.

Meg

Despite the dark and difficult realities documented by this book, it is also true that the pandemic opened the eyes of many to the poverty and inequality present in contemporary Britain. At least for a time, it focused national and political attention on the need to 'build back better' and to 'level up'. It also opened a space for strong narratives about the injustices of poverty to emerge, a space in which the stories and experiences of Covid Realities participants (and others) might be heard. At some points during the first year of the pandemic, there were reasons to hope that the pandemic could signal a turning point, after which things might begin to change for the better.

At the time of writing, however, in the Spring of 2022, the future looks incredibly difficult for families in poverty. This afterword documents how, despite repeated opportunities to support families through the October 2021 and March 2022 Budgets, and at other times too, the government failed to listen or to act. These failures became heightened as we emerged from the pandemic, not to the promised building back better but headlong into a cost-of-living crisis, and to a war in Ukraine, which placed even more pressure on fuel and food prices.

"There was a possibility he would hear us shouting"

On 27 October 2021, almost exactly 18 months since the first UK lockdown began, Chancellor Rishi Sunak delivered his much-anticipated Autumn Budget. Campaigning under a 'keep the lifeline' slogan, charities, politicians (including former Conservative Department for Work and Pensions ministers), and parents and carers taking part in Covid Realities had all spent months calling on the government to do the right thing and keep the £20 increase to Universal Credit, while also extending it to legacy benefits.

Their message was clear: families needed help and the need was becoming ever more urgent. But, instead, the £20 increase was swept away and financial support increased only for claimants in paid work. This was all justified by politicians with tired arguments about the need to prioritise support for 'working families'. A continuation of harmful and inaccurate stereotypes of deserving and undeserving populations, then, ignoring the unpaid work involved in parenting and caring, and the needs of people with health conditions and disabilities. A deliberate and callous missed opportunity to help families facing a cold and difficult winter in the midst of a global pandemic. It seemed that the promise to build back better was nothing more than empty words.

By Spring 2022, families were facing crisis layered upon crisis. Dramatic increases to energy bills and fast-rising food prices were accompanied by National Insurance and tax rises. This difficult context was made even more challenging by stagnating wages and benefit levels that failed to keep pace with inflation. Families that even before the pandemic had very little (if any) slack in their household budgets for additional costs – a situation made worse by COVID-19 – had to somehow now find the resources to cope with spiralling heating, food and transport prices, with predictions of even worse to come.

We had closed the Covid Realities diaries in July 2021. The emerging cost-of-living crisis made the whole team (participants and researchers alike) rethink that decision, and diaries were reopened for the winter of 2021/22. This generated a damning account of what happened when families were left to weather the incoming storm alone. Aurora wrote of this time:

> To cut costs we go without heating. There is quite simply nothing left to cut back on. Our food spend has become minimal.

Lexie set out how the sharply rising costs, and lack of support, left her feeling:

> I am exhausted, how are we meant to deal with Christmas and general living when the £20 uplift has been taken away, the cost of energy has shot through the roof … How do the government expect us to manage all this? Where is the help? Where is the support? Where is the care?

The care that Lexie sought was hard to find. Another Budget came in March 2022: another chance to help, another missed opportunity. The only targeted support for families in poverty was an increase in discretionary support through local authorities. Cross-party calls to increase benefits in line with inflation were dismissed, leading to a historic fall in the real value of benefits at a time when support was so urgently required. As Sunak stood at the despatch box, he was greeted with a cry of "Is that it?" from the opposition benches. Families in poverty felt let down and ignored, yet again. Jo wrote a blog setting out her reaction to the Spring 2022 Budget:

> I've tried so hard over the last few years to find balance financially, emotionally and mentally. The exhaustion of having to count every penny has seriously impacted daily living and there have been times I've been close to sheer panic as I used my bank card. This isn't unfamiliar to me or to millions of other people in the UK.
>
> On Wednesday 23rd March 2022, I, along with so many others, listened to the Chancellor's Spring Statement. Truthfully, I wasn't holding out much hope, but there was a possibility he would hear us shouting from here.
>
> After a cold and painful winter we are bracing ourselves for huge increases in our energy bills amongst other crises. I had hoped Sunak's statement would bring the relief we all need as we career from crisis to crisis: children hungry and cold; parents missing meals; pensioners facing desolate choices between heating their home or eating and so much more.
>
> The statement offered nothing, no hope to those of us on the lowest incomes. We remain trapped in financial prisons with our means of escape blocked by a government unwilling to help us. We all saw, in the pandemic, that the government was willing to spend money, and on a massive scale. And now, we can all see the money being held back when we need it most, and above all, we can see that there is nothing we can do to stop them unless we come together to challenge what is patently wrong.

Although not feeling very hopeful, Jo had nonetheless still been holding on to the possibility that those in charge were listening and had heard the message being broadcast by families like hers: something needed to be done. The political actions, however, suggested otherwise.

What are the consequences of not listening to voices like Jo's? Policy choices based on stereotypes, not on real people and real lives, and the human cost of economic decisions. Policy choices grounded not in evidence, but in ideology – clearly apparent in both the Autumn 2021 and Spring 2022 Budgets. Lives lived on the margins, as Florrie wrote:

> It's like living on the edge of society. You can see normal life courtesy of the TV etc but you're not taking part. You're stigmatised because you're poor and you are demoralised too. You feel worthless. You haven't a voice. The tabloids demonise the poor, we are all feckless, addicts, immoral (their words!) scroungers etc. Reminds me of the novels by Dickens, I'm waiting for the reopening of workhouses!

Policy-making that actually works with the evidence, instead of against it, would not have pressed ahead with cuts to Universal Credit and Working Tax Credits estimated to push around half a million adults and 300,000 children into poverty, while being aware of the potential longer-term health, social and educational consequences of this decision. There is a distinct failure to engage with evidence in a policy-making approach that sees politicians content to talk up promises to 'level up' mental health, while standing by as families struggle, ignoring the reality that poverty and financial insecurity are intrinsically linked to mental ill-health.

The psychologist Abraham Maslow has spoken of humans having a 'hierarchy of needs', meaning that only once basic needs such as warmth, food and safety are met can people concentrate on social and emotional fulfilment and on achieving their potential. Participants in Covid Realities repeatedly describe the exhausting balancing act they face of managing energy, housing and food costs, plus navigating the social security system itself, leaving little time for anything else. Participants like Florrie, Jo and Lexie all describe a feeling not of living but of existing, which all too often has harmful effects on mental health. There is a moral case for providing a more caring social security system that properly supports those who are experiencing hard times. But there is also an economic one. It makes little sense to leave people so caught up in day-to-day survival that there is little room to think of anything else. We all lose out when people are forced to live like this. Social security should be a safety net for us all at difficult times but, done properly, it can also be an investment in families and in the future.

"I know that we can come together to create change"

During the first year of the pandemic, and since, there have been multiple missed opportunities to support families living in poverty, opportunities which we have highlighted in this book. There has rightly been shock and no small amount of disgust at the failure to offer any meaningful protection to families in these difficult times. Promises that 'we are doing all we can' clash starkly with a refusal to place adequate social security support at the heart of the policy response.

There have also been missed opportunities to listen, with people in poverty left feeling that those with the power to change policies perhaps simply do not want to hear what they have to say. This is both difficult and frustrating but it should not deter us from the idea that change is possible. The work that Covid Realities participants have done to amplify the voices of lived experience and to change the narrative around social security and poverty is one example of how we can start to make a difference.

Challenging the harmful stereotypes that underpin current social security policy-making is key to embarking on the longer-term, ambitious work that is needed to tackle inequalities and to make sure that all families have enough income to secure a decent standard of living. Doing so – as Covid Realities participants have said – requires us to recognise our common humanity, and that any one of us could fall on hard times. Not allowing ourselves to be divided up into 'workers' and 'shirkers', but working together on what needs to come next.

We can – and must – demand that policy-makers are held accountable for the decisions they make – decisions that have an enormous impact on the lives of millions of people. We must not allow policy to be made and justified on the basis of spurious arguments and false stereotypes. Instead, we can choose to invest in families and the future. It is possible to hope, care and create change together. This may be the end of a year like no other, but it is not the end of the story. As Jo puts it:

> However hard times are, I know that we can come together to create change and that keeps me fighting. The Covid Realities project has taught me that we deserve to be heard and we will bring about change. Most important of all, I am not alone.

Acknowledgements

There are always lots of people to thank when writing a book, and this is especially the case when there have been many writers.

Most of all, though, we need to thank the participants in Covid Realities, who have worked with us over two years to document and share their experiences of life on a low income during a pandemic. They are collaborators on this book itself, and it (and indeed the wider project) is only possible because of them. We are immeasurably thankful for their input, ideas and energy. Thank you.

We would also like to say a very big thank you to the wider Covid Realities project team. This includes fantastic colleagues at the never-more-needed charity, Child Poverty Action Group (Jane Ahrends, Hannah Aldridge, Lizzie Flew, Alison Garnham, Sophie Howes, Kelly-Marie Jones, Dan Norris, Sara Ogilvie, Bea Pitel, Toral Shah), and colleagues at the University of York not involved in this book (Nicola Moody, Rosalie Warnock). Special thanks to Teresa Frank who has supported the whole project and done vital work to keep it going and on track. We have also been incredibly lucky to work with some fantastic artists – big thanks here go to Hannah Ellison, Laura Lindow, Hector MacInnes and Jean McEwan. Right at the start of this project we commissioned the one and only Tom Flannery to build our website and support the project infrastructure. This was one of our best project decisions and he's been around ever since, designing illustrations, improving our website and contributing to wider project decisions. Pandemic research projects are peculiar things, but this Covid Realities team kept us all on track!

Throughout the project, we have faced difficult decisions, and here we have been so grateful for an engaged and active advisory board. Thanks to all of our advisory board members: Debbie Abrahams MP, Sara Bailey, Alex Beer, Mike Brewer, Sydnie Corley, Catherine Hale, Donald Hirsch, John Hudson, Imran Hussain, Peter Kelly, Grainne McKeever, Clare McNeil, Maggie O'Neill, Iain Porter, Karen Rowlingson, Elaine Squires, Maria Thompson, Sharon Wright, Ros Wynne Jones and Wanda Wyporska.

The Covid Realities project is funded by the Nuffield Foundation, and we are so grateful to the Foundation for making this work possible. We'd especially like to thank Alex Beer, who has been an involved and enthusiastic funder, providing invaluable input across the project. The Nuffield Foundation is an independent charitable trust with a mission to advance social well-being. It funds research that informs social policy, primarily in education, welfare and justice. It also funds student programmes that provide opportunities for young people to develop skills in quantitative and scientific methods. The Nuffield Foundation is the founder and co-funder of the Nuffield Council on Bioethics and the Ada Lovelace Institute. We emphasise that while the Nuffield Foundation has funded this project, the views expressed are those of the authors and not necessarily the Foundation.

As we neared the beginning of the beginning of the end of writing this book we were grateful for thoughtful feedback from several people. Their feedback helped us to steer the book to submission, though remaining errors are (of course) ours alone. Big thanks here to Cathy Bury, Howard Bury, Paul Kaufman, Tina Kaufman, Owen Lewis, Matt Lewis, Kate Pickett and Holly Shaw.

Working on a project of this shape and size and in a pandemic is no easy task and, as a team of authors, we've each faced challenges along the way. We've been thankful here for the unstinting support of our friends and family, which has meant everything at a difficult time. We'd like to give a special shout out to: Calum Patrick Bell, Craig, Felix, Biscuit, Mika, Katie, Liam, Martin and Nina Bell, Kat, Viv and Noa Kaufman, Sky Duthie and John Pybus.

Finally, in the course of making this book (and working on Covid Realities) two children have been born to members of the project team: our production babies. Welcome to this strange world Astrid Power and Astrid Bosworth-Howes (collaboration among the Covid Realities team obviously extends to baby name choices too!) We really hope for a better future for you both.

Ruth, Maddy, Kayleigh, Geoff, Jim, Katie
December 2021

Notes

Foreword
[1] Seldom Seen Kid (street artist).

Introduction
[1] Throughout this book we use the term 'racially minoritised' in place of the more common 'BAME' or 'ethnic minorities'. To speak of minoritisation emphasises that this is a social process shaped by relations of power. It acknowledges, as researchers Adrienne Milner and Sandra Jumbe write, 'that people are actively minoritised by others rather than naturally existing as a minority, as the terms racial minorities or ethnic minorities imply'. See Milner, A. and Jumbe, S. (2020) Using the right words to address racial disparities in COVID-19. *The Lancet. Public Health*, 5 (8): e419–e420.
[2] The personal reflections in the Introduction come from Ruth. Ruth lives in Bradford with her partner and their four young children.
[3] Hall, S.-M. et al (2017) *Intersecting Inequalities: The Impact of Austerity on Black and Minority Ethnic Women in the UK*. London: Women's Budget Group and The Runnymede Trust with RECLAIM and Coventry Women's Voices.
[4] De Agostini, P., Hills, J. and Sutherland, H. (2018) Were we really all in it together? The distributional effects of the 2010–15 UK Coalition Government's tax–benefit policy changes. *Social Policy & Administration*, 52 (5): 929–49.
[5] Benjamin, A. (2013) Poor families facing a 'triple whammy' of benefits, support and service cuts, *The Guardian*, 13 December, www.theguardian. com/society/2011/dec/13/poor-families-triple-whammy-cuts
[6] Clarke, J. and Newman, J. (2012) The alchemy of austerity. *Critical Social Policy*, 32 (3): 299–319.
[7] Jensen, T. and Tyler, I. (2015) 'Benefits broods': the cultural and political crafting of anti-welfare commonsense. *Critical Social Policy*, 35 (4): 470–491.
[8] Garnham, A. (2020) After the pandemic. *IPPR Progressive Review*, https:// onlinelibrary.wiley.com/doi/10.1111/newe.12189
[9] BBC News (2021) Life expectancy falling in parts of England before pandemic – study. *BBC*, 13 October, www.bbc.co.uk/news/uk-58893328; Rashid, T., Bennett, J.E., Paciorek, C.J., Doyle, Y., Pearson-Stuttard, J., Flaxman, S., Fecht, D. et al (2021) Life expectancy and risk of death in 6791 communities in England from 2002 to 2019: high-resolution

spatiotemporal analysis of civil registration data. *The Lancet. Public Health*, 6 (11): e805–e816.

10 Gardam, T. (2020) *How should the Nuffield Foundation research community respond to the social implications of the coronavirus pandemic?* London: Nuffield Foundation, 12 March, www.nuffieldfoundation.org/news/opinion/how-should-the-nuffield-foundation-research-community-respond-to-the-social-implications-of-the-coronavirus-covid-19-pandemic

11 Mass Observation (nd) *Recording Everyday Life in Britain*, www.massobs.org.uk/

12 Participants in Covid Realities come from all four constituent nations of the UK, and the only criteria for getting involved were that participants had dependent children and self-identified as being on a low income. Across 2020 and 2021, 172 parents and carers signed up, with 120 logging at least one diary entry and 47 posting ten or more.

Chapter 1

1 Partington, R. (2020) Price of high-demand food bought online in UK rises sharply, *The Guardian*, 16 April, www.theguardian.com/world/2020/apr/16/price-of-high-demand-food-in-uk-rises-sharply

2 Whitehead, M., Barr, B. and Taylor-Robinson, D. (May 2020) Covid-19: we are not 'all in it together' – less privileged in society are suffering the brunt of the damage. *BMJ Opinion*, 22 May, https://blogs.bmj.com/bmj/2020/05/22/Covid-19-we-are-not-all-in-it-together-less-privileged-in-society-are-suffering-the-brunt-of-the-damage/

3 The personal reflections in this chapter are from Kayleigh, who lives in County Durham with her husband, Craig.

4 *The Economist* (2020) Why Britain is more geographically unequal than any other rich country, 1 August, www.economist.com/britain/2020/07/30/why-britain-is-more-geographically-unequal-than-any-other-rich-country

5 Providing detailed demographic information was not a requirement of taking part in Covid Realities. We wanted to give people freedom to disclose as much (or as little) about themselves as they wanted. Not having demographic detail for all participants means we are unable to draw comparisons between our participants, or even to fully describe who took part. But for us, giving people choice was more important, and is central to the overall ethos of the project.

6 Universal Credit is replacing six benefits called 'legacy benefits'. These are: Housing Benefit; income-related Employment and Support Allowance (ESA); income-based Jobseeker's Allowance (JSA); Child Tax Credits (CTC); Working Tax Credits (WTC) and Income Support.

7 Collinson, A. (2020) The government must ensure no one is paid below the minimum wage due to the furlough scheme. Trades Union Congress blog, 3 November, www.tuc.org.uk/blogs/government-must-ensure-no-one-paid-below-minimum-wage-due-furlough-scheme

8 Sandor, A. (2021) *What the First Covid-19 Lockdown Meant for People in Insecure, Poor Quality Work.* Joseph Rowntree Foundation, 31 March,

www.jrf.org.uk/report/what-first-Covid-19-lockdown-meant-people-insecure-poor-quality-work

9 Clery, E., Dewar, L. and Papoutsaki, D. (2021) Caring without sharing: Single parents' journeys through the COVID-19 pandemic, www.gingerbread.org.uk/policy-campaigns/publications-index/caring-without-sharing-final-report/

10 Office for National Statistics (2021) Mapping loneliness during the coronavirus pandemic, 7 April, www.ons.gov.uk/peoplepopulation andcommunity/wellbeing/articles/mappinglonelinessduringthe coronaviruspandemic/2021-04-07

11 Independent Food Aid Network (2020) *Independent Food Bank Emergency Food Parcel Distribution in the UK February to November 2019 and 2020*, 22 December, https://www.foodaidnetwork.org.uk/ifan-data-since-covid-19

12 Patrick, R., Power, M., Garthwaite, K., Corley, S. and Page, G. (2020) Covid-19 and everyday experiences of hardship: why charitable provision is not enough. *BMJ Opinion*, 21 December, https://blogs.bmj.com/bmj/2020/12/21/covid-19-and-everyday-experiences-of-hardship-why-charitable-provision-is-not-enough/

13 Marshall, C. (2020) Food banks in Scotland call for cash first approaches in the face of uncertain future. Independent Food Aid Network, 20 October, www.foodaidnetwork.org.uk/blog/food-banks-in-scotland-call-for-cash-first-approaches-in-the-face-of

Chapter 2

1 The personal reflections in this chapter are from Jim. Jim lives in Sheffield with his wife, Kat, and their two young children.

2 Wilcock, M. (2020) The soaring cost of Eat Out To Help Out: Rishi Sunak's discount scheme to help pubs and restaurants cost taxpayers £849 million – 70% OVER its £500 million estimate – after 49,000 firms claimed for more than 160 million meals in August, *Daily Mail*, 25 November, www.dailymail.co.uk/news/article-8985597/Rishi-Sunaks-Eat-Help-discount-scheme-cost-taxpayers-849million-70-budget.html

3 Refuge (2021) A year of lockdown: Refuge releases new figures showing dramatic increase in activity, 23 March, https://www.refuge.org.uk/a-year-of-lockdown/

4 Fahmy, E., Williamson, E. and Pantazis, C. (2016) 'Evidence and Policy Review: Domestic Violence and Poverty'. Joseph Rowntree Foundation.

5 Dickens, J. (2020) Suspended head Pauline Wood defends comments about teachers, *Schoolsweek*, https://schoolsweek.co.uk/head-suspended-for-potentially-disparaging-remarks-about-teachers-hits-out/

6 Wootton, D. (2020) Coronavirus is now an excuse not to do anything difficult – but this lazy caution is damaging kids' school, *The Sun*, 20 August, www.thesun.co.uk/news/12457373/dan-wootton-coronavirus-excuse-lazy-caution-kids-school/

7   Although there is a strong association between unemployment and poverty, having paid work is not a guaranteed route out of poverty. 'In-work poverty' or 'working poverty' refers to households living in poverty where at least one person is in employment or self-employment.

8   McNeil, C. et al (2021) *No Longer 'Managing': The Rise of Working Poverty and Fixing Britain's Broken Social Settlement.* IPPR / Covid Realities, www.ippr.org/research/publications/no-longer-managing-the-rise-of-working-poverty-and-fixing-britain-s-broken-social-settlement

9   Blanchflower, D., Costa, R. and Machin, S. (2017) The return of falling real wages. *CEP Real Wages Updates,* 6, https://cep.lse.ac.uk/pubs/download/rwu006.pdf

10   Gaunt, C. (2020) Low pay forces early years workers to quit jobs they love, 21 February, https://www.nurseryworld.co.uk/news/article/low-pay-forces-early-years-workers-to-quit-jobs-they-love

11   Marmot, M. et al (2020) *Build Back Fairer: The COVID-19 Marmot Review. The Pandemic, Socioeconomic and Health Inequalities in England.* Institute of Health Equity, www.health.org.uk/sites/default/files/upload/publications/2020/Build-back-fairer-the-COVID-19-Marmot-review.pdf

12   BBC. (2020) *Coronavirus: They tell us it's a great leveller... it's not | Emily Maitlis | @BBC Newsnight – BBC.* [Online]. YouTube. Available at: https://www.youtube.com/watch?v=L6wIcpdJyCI [Accessed 31 August 2021].

13   Milne, A. (2020) UK under fire for suggesting coronavirus 'great leveller.' [Online]. 9 April. Available at: https://www.reuters.com/article/us-health-coronavirus-leveller-trfn-idUSKCN21R30P [Accessed 31 August 2021]

14   Stewart, H. and Mason, R. (2020) Boris Johnson to stay in hospital amid concerns over political vacuum. *The Guardian.* [Online]. 7 April. Available at: http://www.theguardian.com/world/2020/apr/07/boris-johnson-to-stay-in-hospital-amid-concerns-over-political-vacuum [Accessed 31 August 2021]

15   Anderson, B. (2006) *Imagined communities: Reflections on the origin and spread of nationalism.* London: Verso Books.

16   James, M. and Valluvan, S. (2020) Coronavirus conjuncture: nationalism and pandemic states. *Sociology,* 54 (6): 1238–1250.

17   For information about what 'no recourse to public funds' (NRPF) means, and the support available, see NRPF Network, www.nrpfnetwork.org.uk/

18   Citizens Advice (2020) *No Recourse to Public Funds: Data and Developments. December 2020 update.* Citizens Advice, www.citizensadvice.org.uk/Global/CitizensAdvice/welfare%20publications/Citizens%20Advice%20NRPF%20briefing%20December%202020.pdf

19   Quoted in Joint Council for the Welfare of Immigrants (2021) The Hostile Environment explained, www.jcwi.org.uk/the-hostile-environment-explained

20   The European Economic Area (EEA) consists of member states of the European Union and three countries from the European Free Trade Association (EFTA): Iceland, Liechtenstein and Norway.

21 Typically 'Zambrano carer' status is given when there is not another parent available who is British. In Mindy's case, her son's father was British. However, in awarding the status various other factors can be taken into account.

22 Berry, A. (2011) The EU after Zambrano: Adrian Berry analyses recent judgment on EU rights of residence. *Socialist Lawyer*, (59): 34–36.

23 Stalford, H. (2018) Benefits, babies and the insignificance of being British. *The Journal of Social Welfare & Family Law*, 40 (3): 370–375.

24 Public Health England (2020) Disparities in the risk and outcomes of COVID-19, https://assets.publishing.service.gov.uk/government/uploads/system/uploads/attachment_data/file/908434/Disparities_in_the_risk_and_outcomes_of_COVID_August_2020_update.pdf

25 Independent SAGE describe themselves as 'a group of scientists who are working; together to provide independent scientific advice to the UK government and public on how to minimise deaths and support Britain's recovery from the COVID-19 crisis': www.independentsage.org/independent-sage/

26 Independent SAGE (2020) Covid-19: racialised stigma and inequalities. Recommendations for promoting social cohesion. Briefing note from Independent SAGE. www.independentsage.org/wp-content/uploads/2021/01/Stigma-and-Inequalities_16–12–20_D6.pdf

Chapter 3

1 The personal reflections in this chapter are from Geoff. Geoff lives in York with his seven-year-old son and their two Labradors.

2 Adams, R. (2021) Number of children on free school meals in England soars to 1.7m. *The Guardian*, 17 June, www.theguardian.com/education/2021/jun/17/number-of-children-on-free-school-meals-in-england-soars-to-17m

3 Patrick, R., Anstey, K., Lee, T. and Power, M. (2021) *Fixing Lunch: The Case for Expanding Free School Meals. A Covid Realities and Child Poverty Action Group Rapid-Response Report*, August, https://cpag.org.uk/sites/default/files/files/policypost/Fixing_Lunch.pdf

4 Action for Children (2021) Three ways we're helping tackle the digital divide, www.actionforchildren.org.uk/blog/three-ways-were-helping-tackle-the-digital-divide/

5 Page, G., Power, M. and Patrick, R. (2021) *Uniform Mistakes: The Costs of Going Back to School*. York: Covid Realities.

6 Grahns, A. (2021) Back to school. School uniform grant 2021: how can I claim £150 and who is eligible? *The Sun*, www.thesun.co.uk/money/14247846/school-uniform-grant-2021-claim-eligibility/

7 Scottish Government (2021) *Help with School Clothing Costs*, www.mygov.scot/clothing-grants

8 Welsh Parliament (2021) *Pupil Development Grant – Access*, https://gov.wales/pupil-development-grant-access

9   Northern Ireland Executive (2021) *School Uniform and Uniform Grants*, www.nidirect.gov.uk/articles/school-uniform-and-uniform-grants

10 The Education (Guidance About the Cost of School Uniforms) Act 2021.

11 Children North East (nd) *Poverty Proofing in a Pandemic – Supporting Children, Families and Schools*, https://children-ne.org.uk/poverty-proofing-in-a-pandemic-supporting-children-families-and-schools/

12 Campbell, C. (2021) Covid: generation of children in England at risk from lost learning, *The Guardian*, 3 June, www.theguardian.com/education/2021/jun/03/covid-generation-children-england-risk-lost-learning-schools

13 Adams, R. and Stewart, H. (2021) Covid could cost children £350bn in earnings due to lost learning, says IFS, *The Guardian*, 1 February, www.theguardian.com/education/2021/feb/01/covid-could-cost-children-350bn-in-earnings-through-lost-learning-says-ifs

14 The Sutton Trust (2019) *Elitist Britain*, The Sutton Trust, www.suttontrust.com/wp-content/uploads/2019/12/Elitist-Britain-2019.pdf

15 Cowan, S. (2021) The COVID decade: the consequences of lost access to education at all levels will be felt for years to come, LSE British Politics and Policy, 26 March, https://blogs.lse.ac.uk/politicsandpolicy/the-covid-decade-education/

Chapter 4

1   Miller, D. (ed) (1995) *Unwrapping Christmas*. Oxford: Oxford University Press.

2   Step Change (2014) *Consultation Response: Financial Capability Strategy for the UK*. www.stepchange.org/Portals/0/documents/media/reports/StepChangeresponseNationalFinancialCapabilityStrategyconsultationOct2014.pdf

3   The personal reflections in this chapter are from Geoff. Geoff lives in York with his seven-year-old son and their two Labradors.

4   Daly, M. and Kelly, G. (2015) *Families and Poverty: Everyday Life on a Low Income*. Bristol: Policy Press; Flint, J. (2010) *Coping Strategies? Agencies, Budgeting and Self-Esteem amongst Low-Income Households*. York: Joseph Rowntree Foundation; Patrick, R. (2014) Working on welfare: findings from a qualitative longitudinal study into the lived experiences of welfare reform in the UK. *Journal of Social Policy*, 43 (4): 705–725.

5   Fair By Design (2021) *The Poverty Premium*, https://fairbydesign.com/wp-content/uploads/2021/06/Fair-By-Design-A4-Summary-Doc_May21.pdf

6   Miller, D. (2017) Christmas: an anthropological lens. *HAU: Journal of Ethnographic Theory*, 7 (3): 409–42.

Chapter 5

1   BBC News (2020) Covid-19: more than 40 countries ban UK arrivals, www.bbc.co.uk/news/uk-55391289

2   Sherwood, H. (2018) Doreen Lawrence: Grenfell tenants faced 'institutional indifference', *The Guardian*, 2 June, www.theguardian.com/society/2018/jun/02/doreen-lawrence-grenfell-tenants-faced-institutional-indifference

3   Lister, R. (2018) From Windrush to Universal Credit – the art of 'institutional indifference', *Open Democracy*, 10 October, www.opendemocracy.net/en/opendemocracyuk/from-windrush-to-universal-credit-art-of-institutional-indifference/

4   Mental Health Foundation (2021) www.mentalhealth.org.uk/statistics/mental-health-statistics-poverty

5   Barr, B. et al (2015) 'First do no harm': Are disability assessments associated with adverse trends in mental health? A longitudinal ecological study. *Journal of Epidemiology & Community Health*, 1–7.

6   Wickham, S., Bentley, L., Rose, T., Whitehead, M., Taylor-Robinson, D. and Barr, B. (2020) Effects on mental health of a UK welfare reform, Universal Credit: a longitudinal controlled study. *The Lancet. Public Health*, 5 (3): e157–e164.

7   Full Fact (2019) Employment: Is employment up only because of zero hours contracts?, https://fullfact.org/economy/employment-since-2010-zhcs/

8   Mind (2020) Mental health facts and statistics, www.mind.org.uk/information-support/types-of-mental-health-problems/statistics-and-fact.s-about-mental-health/how-common-are-mental-health-problems/

9   NatCen (2021) *Society Watch 2021: Mental Health, Should We Be Worried?* www.natcen.ac.uk/media/2050456/Society-Watch-2021-MentalHealth-Should-We-Be-Worried.pdf

10   Masterton, W., Carver, H. and Parkes, T. (2020) Parks and green spaces are important for our mental health – but we need to make sure that everyone can benefit. *The Conversation*, https://theconversation.com/parks-and-green-spaces-are-important-for-our-mental-health-but-we-need-to-make-sure-that-everyone-can-benefit-142322

11   Office for National Statistics (2021) How has lockdown changed our relationship with nature?, www.ons.gov.uk/economy/environmental accounts/articles/howhaslockdownchangedourrelationshipwithnature/2021–04–26

12   The personal reflections in this chapter are from Katie. Katie lives in York with her husband, a pub landlord.

13   Office for National Statistics (2021) How has lockdown changed our relationship with nature?, www.ons.gov.uk/economy/environmental accounts/articles/howhaslockdownchangedourrelationshipwithnature/2021–04–26

14   Office for National Statistics (2021) Coronavirus and depression in adults, Great Britain, January to March 2021, www.ons.gov.uk/peoplepopulation andcommunity/wellbeing/articles/coronavirusanddepressioninadultsgreat britain/januarytomarch2021

15   BBC News (2021) Households 'buy 3.2 million pets in lockdown', www.bbc.co.uk/news/business-56362987

16 Tyler, I. and Slater, T. (2018) Rethinking the sociology of stigma. *The Sociological Review Monographs*, 66 (4): 721–43.

17 CNBC (2020) How Zoom became so popular during social distancing, www.cnbc.com/2020/04/03/how-zoom-rose-to-the-top-during-the-coronavirus-pandemic.html

18 Lister, R. (2015) 'To count for nothing': poverty beyond the statistics. *Journal of the British Academy*, 3: 139–65, www.thebritishacademy.ac.uk/documents/1563/05_Lister_1817.pdf

19 Power, A. and Benton, E. (2021) Where next for Britain's 4,300 mutual aid groups? *LSE Policy & Politics* blog, 6 May, https://blogs.lse.ac.uk/Covid19/2021/05/06/where-next-for-britains-4300-mutual-aid-groups/

20 Gov.UK (2021) Vaccinations in the UK, https://coronavirus.data.gov.uk/details/vaccinations

21 Mohdin, A. et al (2021) Vaccine hesitancy narrative fuelling divisions in Bolton, says MP. *The Guardian*, 18 May, www.theguardian.com/world/2021/may/18/vaccine-hesitancy-narrative-fuelling-divisions-in-bolton-says-mp

22 Department of Health and Social Care (2021) Mental health recovery plan backed by £500 million, www.gov.uk/government/news/mental-health-recovery-plan-backed-by-500-million

23 Savage, M. (2021) Raise benefits to curb UK crisis in mental health, expert urges, *The Guardian*, 21 March, www.theguardian.com/politics/2021/mar/21/raise-benefits-to-curb-uk-crisis-in-mental-health-expert-urges

Chapter 6

1 Francis-Devine, B., Powell, A. and Clark, H. (2021) *Coronavirus Job Retention Scheme: Statistics*. House of Commons Library Briefing.

2 HM Treasury (2020) The Chancellor Rishi Sunak provides an updated statement on coronavirus, 20 March, www.gov.uk/government/speeches/the-chancellor-rishi-sunak-provides-an-updated-statement-on-coronavirus

3 Brewer, M., Handscomb, K. and Shah, K. (2021) In need of support? Lessons from the COVID-19 crisis for our social security system. Resolution Foundation, www.resolutionfoundation.org/app/uploads/2021/04/In-need-of-support.pdf; Brewer, M. and Handscomb, K. (2021) Half-measures: the chancellor's options for Universal Credit in the budget. Resolution Foundation, www.resolutionfoundation.org/publications/half-measures

4 Waters, T. and Wernham, T. (2021) *The Expiry of the Universal Credit Uplift: Impacts and Policy Options*. Institute for Fiscal Studies, July, https://ifs.org.uk/publications/15528

5 In response to this decision two disabled people claiming ESA launched a legal challenge, with a hearing held over two days at the High Court in September 2021. At the time of submitting this manuscript (December 2021) they were still awaiting the decision.

6   Pring, J. (2021) Universal Credit 'basic fairness' £20 uplift case given High Court go-ahead, *Disability News*, 6 May, www.disabilitynewsservice.com/universal-credit-basic-fairness-20-uplift-case-given-high-court-go-ahead/

7   de Vries, R., Geiger, B.B., Scullion, L., Summers, K., Edmiston, D., Gibbons, A., Ingold, J., Robertshaw, D. and Young, D (2021) Solidarity in a crisis? Trends in attitudes to benefits during COVID-19, www.distantwelfare.co.uk/attitudes

8   Savage, M. (2021) Don't slash Covid benefit uplift, former Tory minister urges, *The Guardian*, 20 June, www.theguardian.com/society/2021/jun/20/dont-slash-covid-benefit-uplift-former-tory-minister-urges

9   Cited in Abraham, E. (2020) How the government have continued to prop up a two-tier welfare state by ignoring 2 million people during this pandemic, *Disability Benefits Consortium*, 2 December, https://disabilitybenefitsconsortium.com/2020/12/02/how-the-government-have-continued-to-prop-up-a-two-tier-welfare-state-by-ignoring-2-million-people-during-this-pandemic/

10 Flint, J. and Powell, R. (eds) (2019) *Class, Ethnicity and State in the Polarized Metropolis: Putting Wacquant to Work*. Basingstoke: Palgrave Macmillan; Garthwaite, K. (2016) *Hunger Pains: Life inside Foodbank Britain*. Bristol: Policy Press; Patrick, R. (2017) *For Whose Benefit? The Everyday Realities of Welfare Reform*. Bristol: Policy Press; Shildrick, T. and MacDonald, R. (2012) *Poverty and Insecurity: Life in Low-Pay, No-Pay Britain*. Bristol: Policy Press.

11 Foster, D. (2019) Britain's austerity has gone from cradle to grave, *Jacobin*, https://jacobinmag.com/2019/04/britain-life-expectancy-austerity-conservative-party-tories; Collinson, P. (2019) Life expectancy falls by six months in biggest drop in UK forecasts, *The Guardian*, 7 March, www.theguardian.com/society/2019/mar/07/life-expectancy-slumps-by-five-months

12 CPAG (2020) *Mind the Gaps: Reporting on Families' Incomes during the Pandemic*. Child Poverty Action Group, https://cpag.org.uk/sites/default/files/files/policypost/CPAG-mind-the-gaps-briefing-28-May.pdf

13 Patrick, R. and Simpson, M. (2020) *Universal Credit Could Be a Lifeline in Northern Ireland, but It Must Be Designed with People Who Use It*. Joseph Rowntree Foundation, https://pure.ulster.ac.uk/en/publications/universal-credit-could-be-a-lifeline-in-northern-ireland-but-it-m

14 Patrick, R. and Lee, T. (2021) Advance to debt paying back benefit debt – what happens when deductions are made to benefit payments? *Covid Realities*, 7 January, https://covidrealities.org/learnings/write-ups/debt-deductions

15 Edwards, Z., Howes, S., Reedy, J. and Sefton, T. (2020) *Poverty in the Pandemic: An Update on the Impact of Coronavirus on Low-income Families and Children*. London: Child Poverty Action Group, The Church of England, https://cpag.org.uk/sites/default/files/files/policypost/Poverty-in-the-pandemic_update.pdf

16 DWP (2021) Universal Credit statistics, 29 April 2013 to 8 July 2021, 21 August, www.gov.uk/government/statistics/universal-credit-statistics-29-april-2013-to-8-july-2021/universal-credit-statistics-29-april-2013-to-8-july-2021

17 Summers, K., Scullion, L., Geiger, B.B., Robertshaw, D., Edmiston, D., Gibbons, A., Karagiannaki, E., de Vries, R. and Ingold, J. (2021) *Claimants' Experiences of the Social Security System during the First Wave of COVID-19.* Project report, Welfare at a (Social) Distance.

18 George Osborne, Conservative Party conference speech, 2010.

19 David Freud (2021) *Clashing Agendas: Inside the Welfare Trap.* London: Nine Elms Books.

20 Patrick, R. (2017) *For Whose Benefit? The Everyday Realities of Welfare Reform.* Bristol: Policy Press.

21 de Vries, R., Geiger, B.B., Scullion, L., Summers, K., Edmiston, D., Gibbons, A., Ingold, J., Robertshaw, D. and Young, D (2021) Solidarity in a crisis? Trends in attitudes to benefits during COVID-19, www.distantwelfare.co.uk/attitudes

22 Wright, S., Fletcher, D.R. and Stewart, A.B.R. (2020) Punitive benefit sanctions, welfare conditionality, and the social abuse of unemployed people in Britain: transforming claimants into offenders? *Social Policy & Administration,* 54 (2): 278–94.

23 Baumberg Geiger, B. et al (2020) *Claiming but Connected to Work. Rapid Report 1.* Welfare at a Social Distance, University of Salford, Salford, www.distantwelfare.co.uk/_files/ugd/e77e1a_58a28e2f58c44f81b97230a83da5d13e.pdf

24 Webster, D. (2022) Benefit Sanctions Statistics, February 2022, 7 March: https://cpag.org.uk/policy-and-campaigns/briefing/david-webster-university-glasgow-briefings-benefit-sanctions

25 Baumberg Geiger, B. et al (2020) *Claiming but Connected to Work. Rapid Report 1.* Welfare at a Social Distance, University of Salford, www.distantwelfare.co.uk/_files/ugd/e77e1a_58a28e2f58c44f81b97230a83da5d13e.pdf

Conclusion

1 Solnit, R. (2016) *Hope in the Dark: Untold Histories, Wild Possibilities.* Chicago, IL: Haymarket Books.

2 Holm, T. (2021) Child poverty now costs Britain £38bn a year, says new independent report, *The Guardian,* 19 September, www.theguardian.com/society/2021/sep/19/child-poverty-now-costs-britain-38bn-a-year-says-new-independent-report

3 Solnit, R. (2016) 'Hope is an embrace of the unknown': Rebecca Solnit on living in dark times, *The Guardian,* 15 July, www.theguardian.com/books/2016/jul/15/rebecca-solnit-hope-in-the-dark-new-essay-embrace-unknown

4 The Care Collective (2020) *The Care Manifesto: The Politics of Interdependence.* London: Verso Books.

5   Sherwood, H. (2018) Doreen Lawrence: Grenfell tenants faced 'institutional indifference', *The Guardian*, 2 June, www.theguardian.com/society/2018/jun/02/doreen-lawrence-grenfell-tenants-faced-institutional-indifference

6   The Care Collective (2020) *The Care Manifesto: The Politics of Interdependence*. London: Verso Books.

7   Crossley, S., Garthwaite, K. and Patrick, R. (2019) *The Fragmentation of Poverty in the UK: What's the Problem? A Working Paper*, www.whatstheproblem.org.uk

8   Adelaine, A. et al (2020) Knowledge is power: an open letter to UKRI, 19 August, https://raceingeography.org/2020/08/19/knowledge-is-power-an-open-letter-to-ukri/

9   Wilkinson, R. and Pickett, K. (2010) *The Spirit Level: Why Equality is Better for Everyone*. London: Penguin Books.

10 Piketty, T. (2014) *Capital in the 21st Century*. Cambridge, MA: Belknap Press.

11 Williams, F. (2016) Critical thinking in social policy: the challenges of past, present and future. *Social Policy & Administration*, 50 (6): 628–47.

12 Levitas, R. (2013) *Utopia as Method: The Imaginary Reconstitution of Society*. Basingstoke: Palgrave Macmillan.

Index